Content Marketing: How to Get Started

THE LITTLE PINK SPOONS METHOD

Lisa Ann Landry

Life On Purpose Publishing
WINDSOR, CONNECTICUT

Content Marketing: How to Get Started

THE LITTLE PINK SPOONS METHOD

Lisa Ann Landry

A Gap Closer ™ Publication

> A Division of Life On Purpose Publishing
> Windsor, Connecticut

Content Marketing: How to Get Started/Lisa Ann Landry

ISBN 10: 0-9961908-4-8

ISBN 13: 978-0-9961908-4-8

Dedication

I remember the look of astonishment on his face the very first time he saw me speak. It was to a crowd of 200 people. Ever since that day he was adamant I had a book in me. This book is dedicated to my husband Counsil Myles Griffin. Thank you for believing in my gifts.

This book is also dedicated to my longtime friend and business partner on many projects, Ann Evanston. In spite of my kicking and screaming and total resistance she introduced me to the power and psychology of social networking. In the beginning it was so foreign to me I didn't even have the vocabulary to ask a question. Look at me now. Thank you for pushing me in this direction; it has changed my life.

Acknowledgements

I wish to thank the following people for their contributions to my inspiration and knowledge. I sincerely appreciate the many ways you aided me in creating this book:

- Ann Evanston, President of Warrior-Preneur
- Dr. Angela Massey, "The Gap Closer"
- Toni Harris "The Turn Around Queen"
- Tarsha Polk "The Marketing Lady"
- The SiSTARS MasterMind: Gena Yuvette Davis, Nikki Woods, Tish Times, Star Bobatoon, Sherry Darden, Tarsha Polk, Toni Harris, and Dr. Angela Massey

Contents

Foreword

When Lisa Ann and I were dating, I knew what she did professionally, but the first time I witnessed it for myself, I had a new profound love and respect for her. She was scheduled to speak at a big conference at this beautiful resort in Tucson, Arizona. We were living in Phoenix at the time, and we thought it could be a nice weekend retreat, so I went along. I doubled as her driver and her date!

The first day of the conference I joined in as a participant. Here I was among a crowd of over 200 people. Lisa Ann walks into the conference and takes charge. If you know her, you know the energy she has that makes everyone focus and be present—in the moment!

The group that I sat with wanted to know who I was; I let them know I was the speaker's guest. I received a welcome that was filled with admiration for being someone special enough to know Lisa Ann and be her special guest. Sometimes being around Lisa Ann is like being around a celebrity!

I remember when Lisa Ann decided it was important to her business and her career to learn as much as she could about social media. I then watched her become a social media marketing expert, traveling throughout the continental U.S., and internationally to provide training and expertise to professionals from hundreds of different companies and corporations.

I mention this because when you read this book, I want you to know you're in great hands! Lisa Ann draws from her education, corporate background, and her experiences as the CEO of Paradigm Shifts Training and Development. She has been instrumental in building the skills and improving the knowledge of the thousands she has trained and coached. Consequently, she helps companies stay competitive. That's how I know this book will help you become a lot savvier in creating content to market your company.

I am fortunate not just because I know Lisa Ann professionally, but because she is my wife and my life partner. I'm so proud of her success over the years. My wish for her is that this book continues to propel her forward so she becomes even more successful, and my wish for you is that this book will propel your business forward to a higher level of success as well.

I'm sure you will learn exactly what you need to know to create the kind of content guaranteed to get the greatest results!

Counsil Myles Griffin, The Husband
Seattle, Washington

Preface

In a good economy I make a great living as a contracted trainer. Since starting my business in 1995, I've never had to market my company. Through word of mouth, I've been able to easily secure contract work. Did I say when the economy is good? In a bad economy *training dollars evaporate.* In February 2009, my training contracts took a nose dive and I went from working 12 to 15 days a month to working 5 sometimes 4 days a month. Normally I panic in these situations but over the years I've learned businesses have peaks and valleys and instead of freaking out it's best to go learn something new. I found myself with free time and so I decided to take a 10-week Social Media Boot Camp while I weathered the (bad economy) storm.

You have to know that I had an incredibly bad attitude about the relevance of social media. I thought social media was stupid and just a passing fad (I've learned many others feel that way too). From the mindset of a small business owner—don't get me started on Farmville, or Dirty Birds, Crazy Birds, or Angry Birds—I don't have time for that! I also thought, "I don't need people to know my business!" (in a disgusted voice). And to think I had to pay for something I thought was stupid! I had no idea how this one program would launch me into an entirely new career field.

The program was called the *Social Networking Boot Camp* created by brilliant and intuitive entrepreneur Ann Evanston. Ann is a longtime friend and business coach. It was 10 weeks of work, including a weekly group conference call with all the participants. It was so hard for me because I felt I was learning a new language. I made it through the boot camp *dazed and confused!* So, being the Type A personality that I am . . . I took it two more times until it began to sink in!

I'm proud of how far I've come, but I want you to understand my expectations so you can appreciate where I am in the social media scheme of things. My business *Paradigm Shifts Training and Development* designs and delivers management and staff development workshops. When my energies are focused on where my talent and passion is (development and delivery) there's little time for marketing and growing my business. I became aware of what social media could do, yet I was skeptical of its promise to help me grow my business.

I had six goals when I attended the boot camp:
1. Develop good social media habits
2. Get followers by increasing my Internet presence
3. Blog
4. Blog comment at least once a week
5. Get business
6. Get found in search engines

When I started the boot camp, although I'm an international trainer, I had no visibility in search engines. Here is what I mean . . . Suppose you saw me speak at a conference on High Impact Communication Skills. I consistently have anywhere from 100 to 200 people in that conference. It's an understatement when I say people absolutely love it. Now, imagine a year or two has passed since you attended the conference and you've been charged with putting together a conference for your company. You think I would be a great fit as a keynote speaker or to conduct a breakout session, but you don't know how to get in touch with me. What do you do? Go to Google like any normal person would and search for Lisa Landry.

In the Google search results, you would have found Lisa Landry the American comedian, actress, and writer. You might have found Jackee Harry, who played Lisa Landry on the comedy series that ran in the late 1990s call *Sister, Sister*.

If, by chance, you forgot my last name and just searched on Lisa Ann you would have found the gorgeous, hot, tanned porn star (totally X-Rated). Can you see the problem here?

Back then I was nowhere close to the first page in search results. If you tried hard, you might have found me on page ten. The only problem with that is nobody looks through ten pages of Google for anything. Many people believe if you are not on the first page of search results you don't exist. Since I didn't exist, I wasn't getting any business and the boot camp was going to help me turn that around.

Ann started pushing me to coach her clients who were going through the boot camp. I say pushed because I was not at all confident in my knowledge or abilities to coach on social media, but she insisted and I began coaching people on the topics I was comfortable with. My coaching assignments increased to the point where the program evolved and Ann and I started partnering on social media projects.

Our partnership led us to develop a Social Networking Coaching Club certification program. We also co-created a program hosted on Udemy.com called *Strategies for Marketing Successfully in Social Media*. You can find that at https://www.udemy.com/strategies-for-marketing-successfully-in-social-media. It has excellent reviews and I'm incredibly proud of it. Eventually, Ann wanted to go in a different direction and sold me the boot camp.

Look at me now! As a result of taking the boot camp I've transformed from a social media know-nothing (so green I couldn't even ask a question) with zero web presence to an international social media strategist, trainer and coach! Now, when you Google search for "Lisa Ann Landry" you will find ten pages of my social profiles and content. Now that prospects can find me I am (giddy) busy, busy, busy!

I am not a social media marketing guru, but I am a social media enthusiast and a master trainer with 30 years of corporate experience. The training opened my perspective and consequently, I started to see the new vision of the future and social media was in it, not just for me, but for everyone. It occurred to me that social media marketing has the biggest promise for entrepreneurs and small business owners.

I've since received an advanced certificate in Social Media from the University of San Francisco and a certificate in Marketing Management from Columbia College. I speak and train at summits, conferences, seminars and on radio talk shows on the topic of Social Media Marketing and specific social sites or topics such as Facebook, LinkedIn, Twitter, YouTube, Google Plus and blogging.

I share my credentials with you, not to impress you, but to impress upon you how getting started with content marketing *now* can change your business just like it changed mine.

Lisa Ann Landry
Seattle, Washington

Introduction

L et's get one thing out of the way before you read one more page of this book"

Social media is not marketing!

Yes, I said that! I'm quite known for saying that! Now, some of you are thinking, "Wait Ann, I just bought this book so I can market my business on social media! What are you talking about Ann?!?"

You are correct. That's exactly my point. Marketing opportunities *are* everywhere. Advertising, radio, TV, press releases, billboards, videos, e-mail automation, speaking, networking, associations, I could go on and on. Social media is just another platform to market . . .

- To show up.

- To build your brand.
- To be known.
- To grow leads, prospects and customers.

These are all things we want marketing to do! That means in every place you market, what matters is determining the best strategy for success on that platform.

With social media marketing, content strategy is the necessary evil (you have probably heard that before, huh?). I have been a content marketer for what seems like forever! That's exactly what the role is as a speaker and facilitator. We share stories, lessons, plans, steps, strategies and knowledge to educate and inspire others:

- To engage
- To increase visibility
- To sell our products and services.

We practice, the *"little pink spoon technique"* which you will learn more about here in Lisa Ann's book and why it's so important. This technique allows you to draw the potential customer—the buyer—in so that they are interested and excited about what you have to offer.

Funny thing? That's where I met Lisa Ann Landry! We were both in a hotel somewhere in the United States, speaking on our platforms, and she walked across the hall and introduced herself. We have been fast friends, "sisters from another mister," and business partners ever since.

As my own business accelerated in 2000, Lisa Ann developed her business by teaching public seminars. Honestly, by 2007, social media, then called social networking, kept us together. I developed the Social Networking Coaching Club, Lisa Ann become a student of it, then a certified coach. In 2011, about.com named me one of the top six marketing consultants. Now, she owns that business and is a top marketer.

Becoming a top marketer is about understanding content strategy. Which means you can become one, too.

Yes, developing content is the necessary evil of your business marketing success, especially if you're choosing social media as the platform you want to market on! What's great about our relationship? Lisa Ann and I have different passions in terms of how we help businesses become successful. My passion is teaching small business owners how to organize their knowledge and truly step into the compelling force they are meant to be. Her passion is showing people how to develop their content strategy for social media and be a compelling force online.

When we started so many years ago, back in 2006, the biggest complaint was, "I don't want to share what I eat, drink, or pictures of my dog!" Well you don't have to. Follow the strategies in Lisa Ann's book. (I will tell you, though—food, dogs and what you drink and eat bring *tons* of likes, friends and followers!)

There is no one better to learn social media marketing from, in my opinion, than Lisa Ann Landry. She eats, breathes, and sleeps it! I can't say that!

Here is what I want you to know: content strategy does not have to be a necessary evil. When you understand the dynamics of consistent replicatable marketing it becomes easy instead of a necessary evil. And within the chapters of this book Lisa Ann will give you exactly that. You will have a plan; you will have content that you can reuse and repurpose, and you will understand where to go when you need to refresh your content marketing.

That means social media can become a powerful marketing platform in your business, like mine. And content strategy is no longer a necessary evil.

So consume this book. Know there is a plan, and you can become a top marketer like Lisa Ann and me.

Know that it becomes the compelling force that attracts leads, builds your relationships, calls your tribe, and closes more sales!

I also believe in the ideas in this book and would love to connect! Share your journey! Like Lisa Ann shares here, I believe in relationship! And you might be surprised to see all the food, drink, relationship and "Earlisms" (my husband, a Facebook marketing content strategy! Oh, you just have to go see to understand!) that will engage you to my tribe!

Ann Evanston
San Pablo, California

Contact Information:

https://twitter.com/AnnEvanston
https://www.facebook.com/AnnEvanston
https://www.facebook.com/WarriorPreneur
http://AnnEvanston.com
http://linkedin/in/AnnEvanston
http://YouTube.com/AEvanston

CHAPTER 1

A Spotlight on What Content Marketing Is

What is content marketing? Take a look at any marketer's toolbox and you'll find that content marketing has been a staple for 175 years! Content marketing is not a new idea. Haven't we always been strategic while creating and distributing relevant and valuable content to our customers? What brings content marketing to a new level is the technologies now available to anyone. These technologies are transforming content marketing.

In fact, content marketing is the most commercially important digital marketing trend in the past few years. Why? First, it's more cost-effective than ever before. Second, there are increasingly more delivery options that appeal to your target market. Today's technology allows you to reach your audience through blogs, social media, e-Newsletters, videos, infographics, mobile apps, and this list goes on. Gone are the days where you were hoping to get publicity through television, radio, and/or newspaper exposure. Today, *you are the new media.* While there are many resources to capture your audience's attention, as an entrepreneur you must know what to do with those resources, when to use them, and how often. Simply put, you cannot afford to waste your time, your money, or your energy.

If you want to improve customer relationships, increase brand loyalty, boost engagement and raise brand awareness, content marketing is the tool that can make that happen. It's time to create a content marketing strategy so that you are creating and distributing valuable, and relevant content to attract, acquire, *and* engage your target audience. In turn, this will generate profitable customer activity for your business.

Content marketing is creating and sharing free valuable content to attract and convert prospects into repeat buyers. While the content you share is closely related to what you sell, it is not promotional nor does it talk directly about a product or company. Content marketing is concerned with providing something of value to customers and prospects.

This book is designed to help you develop a strategy to overcome the challenges of creating engaging content that connects and appeals to your customers on a consistent and regular basis. Knowing what content marketing is and knowing how to harness its power will catapult your company to a level of success you have not achieved previously. The key is *knowing* what to do and what not to do, so read on.

Don't Be Salesy, Pushy, Slimy, Sleazy

Have you ever been spammed while visiting a social site? Of course, you have! I want you to think about how it felt. If you're not yet using social sites, you'll need an example. I'm a true-blue IBM PC kind of chick. Perhaps it's because I worked for IBM for nearly 14 years. Consequently, I was living life mighty fine with no Apple (curse word at IBM) products.

One birthday my husband gifted me with an iPad. Boy was I disabled when I got it! I found out quickly it didn't work anything like IBM products. However, once I got through my learning curve, I was so delighted I started posting on my social sites: "I got a new iPad for my birthday, and now I don't have to carry books, papers, Power-Point, etc." As soon as I used the word *iPad*, I started getting spammed. I even tried to be slick and spell iPad wrong EYEtHAD— that didn't fool anybody. I still got spammed!

Imagine how it feels to be constantly interrupted with sales messages like: "You have just won a new iPad" or "You have just won a gift certificate for a new iPad." Because we are not on social sites to receive those kinds of messages, we feel intruded upon and violated. To put it bluntly, this kind of intrusion ticks people off! When people get ticked off, do you know what they do? Many people simply disconnect from the offender. They use that X button . . . delete . . . trash—well, you get my point. Others simply ignore you. Either choice is bad business for an enterprising entrepreneur.

Now, answer this question: When you decide to disconnect from someone on a social site, do you notify that person ahead of time? No! Here is your takeaway: When your brand is too pushy, salesy, slimy, and sleazy using the social sites, you will tick off your friends, fans, prospects, and followers. They will unfriend, unfan *(I made that word up)*, and unfollow you. They may even report you as a spammer. Losing those connections can be costly to your brand. On the other hand, when you share valuable, relevant content and share your knowledge, wisdom and expertise, you educate your target market about your products and services. This process allows you to build a relationship with your readers that help them to know, like, and trust your brand.

The Law of Reciprocity

Are you having trouble wrapping your head around giving away your knowledge and wisdom? You can do this as long as you remember the goal. The goal is to figure out how to educate people *and* attract them to your content, so they think, "Wow! This person is connecting with and talking to me. I need to know more. They get me; they get what it is I'm up against."

As a consultant and coach paid for my knowledge and wisdom, I also had trouble with the idea of giving away my knowledge and wisdom. I worked 14 years at IBM where I learned many powerful lessons. One lesson I learned the hard way was in a competitive corporate environment, you must be cautious of freely giving your knowledge and wisdom. Some people have no scruples and will do anything to succeed, even if it means hurting someone else. While it's unfortunate, a peer may steal your idea and present it as his or hers *and* get promoted over you (*that happened to me a couple of times*). Those experiences taught me several lessons:

- Protect my knowledge
- Be strategic when deciding to share my knowledge
- Carefully choose whom to share my knowledge with so that I benefit or profit with a promotion or award

I suppose you could say I became a victim of that competitive corporate mindset. It took hard work for me to shake off that conditioning and instead embrace the Law of Reciprocity in social media. The Law of Reciprocity is about giving or sharing your knowledge, wisdom, and expertise with others. You do so with an open heart to serve and aid your community with the underlying belief the same energy you put out will somehow be returned to you. Start to pay attention to other people's content and interactions in the social space; you will recognize those who operate with the Law of Reciprocity mindset.

Practicing the Law of Reciprocity is the first step in getting grounded in the concept of education-based marketing. As an entrepreneur, your goal is to achieve credibility, influence and trust on the Internet with the intention of creating raving fans. These are customers who not only buy your products and services but tell others. You can make that happen by using what I call the Baskin-Robbins method of education-based marketing.

"No one ever becomes poor by giving." Anne Frank

Baskin-Robbins Little Pink Spoons

At Baskin-Robbins, there are baskets of little pink spoons (LPS) all over the store. Those little pink spoons are strategically placed throughout to entice you (Baskin-Robbins' target market) to sample their flavors. You have never been to a Baskin-Robbins store and heard, while sampling their ice cream, "Sorry. You've reached your limit. I'm cutting you off."

How fascinating! Baskin-Robbins won't give you a free gallon of ice cream, but they will give you a gallon's worth of little pink spoons hoping to entice you to buy a gallon or

31. Actually, they prefer you buy 31 gallons and have a party where you invite all your friends and share the ice cream. When you do that, you turn into Baskin-Robbins' marketing force.

One of the easiest places to do education-based marketing (content marketing) is through blogging. It is the non-salesy way for people to learn about you and your products or services. It is a smart and easy way to build credibility and trust. Here's the bonus: It is the easiest way to dominate search engines!

Think of your blog as the gallon of ice cream in the Baskin-Robbins analogy. Creating content is time-consuming; however, once you put in the time why not leverage it by sprinkling little pink spoons (LPS) of juicy morsels of goodness from your blog around to the other social platforms you're using? Blogging is a great foundation for your social media work, and it is not the only source for little pink spoons.

Remember, with the Law of Reciprocity when you give your knowledge, wisdom, and expertise to your community, you're not giving away the whole gallon. You're just giving away little pink spoons (LPS) from your gallon of ice cream. It's these little pink spoons of enticing juicy morsels of valuable, relevant content that inspire them to pay for the whole gallon.

As previously mentioned, it is important to understand that your fans, customers, and prospects hate spam and push marketing. Many brands use the social sites to do traditional push or interruption marketing and quite frankly, it irritates people! Consequently, fans disconnect from brands when this happens. Be clear, when someone disconnects, they are not going to call you first to let you know they are kicking you to the curb. Instead of push marketing, use inbound marketing or what I call education-based marketing techniques like the Baskin-Robbins little pink spoon (LPS) method.

Content Marketing Benefits

Here is a list of content marketing's benefits for entrepreneurs:

1. It's more cost effective than traditional marketing by as much as 62% less costly
2. The content you produce establishes you as a thought leader (regarded as an authority in your industry)—positioning you to influence your target market to act
3. The high-quality content you produce builds awareness of your brand and high levels of authority, trust and respect from your target audience
4. Your high-quality content attracts others to link to it which increases your authority and your search engine optimization

5. When you give your target audience the kind of content they want (video, infographics, case studies, how-to's, etc.) engagement increases
6. Your sites get increased traffic because your high-quality, relevant content soothes your target audience's pain points:

    - Satisfy a need
    - Deliver a service
    - Reduce stress
    - Emotionally satisfy

Summary

The Baskin-Robbins analogy is at the heart of content marketing. So content marketing means creating and sharing free valuable content to attract and convert prospects into customers, and customers into repeat buyers. The type of content you share is closely related to what you sell. Baskin-Robbins is not sharing little pink spoons (LPS) of marbles. In other words, the goal of content marketing is to educate people so that they know, like, and trust you enough to do business with you. When you go to Baskin-Robbins, there is no one at the door loudly and forcefully promoting the sale on the chocolate raspberry swirl. That means your content will rarely be promotional and seldom talk directly about a product or company. Content marketing is more concerned with providing something of value to customers and prospects.

Read on to learn how to reap the benefits of content marketing.

CHAPTER 2

The Content Marketing Imperative

The content marketing imperative is about getting found by your prospects and clients. When people go to the Internet looking for information and they find great content—not salesy content—Google wants it to rank well in the search results so those people can find it. This is good for your business, product and service.

One of the best ways to generate presence in search results is through content marketing by using what I've described as the Baskin-Robbins Little Pink Spoon Method (LPS) as outlined in chapter one. Make it your goal to use the Baskin-Robbins LPS method to educate your target market and entice them with juicy morsels of valuable, relevant content.

Remember our previous discussion about your blog? One of the easiest places to start with content marketing is your blog. Think of your blog as your very own online site where you can write a diary, a newspaper, a journal, even a magazine on topics relevant to your target market. Fill it with content of varying lengths and types that your target market wants to consume such as video, audio, pictures, infographics, etc. When your target market finds your juicy content, they share it, and that's how it spreads.

Content Spreads to Create Potent Exposure

Here is an excellent case study on how a few raving fans can cause your brand message to spread and impact thousands of people. Further, it demonstrates how quickly content spreads to create potent exposure.

The Wizarding World of Harry Potter Case Study

"Imagine you're the head of marketing at a theme park, and you're charged with announcing a major new attraction. What would you do?

Well, the old rules of marketing suggest that you pull out your wallet. You'd probably spend millions to buy your way into people's minds, interrupting them with TV spots, billboards by the side of the highway, and other "creative" Madison Avenue advertising techniques.

You'd also hire a big PR agency, who would beg the media to write about your attraction.

The traditional PR approach requires a self-congratulatory press release replete with company muckety-mucks claiming that the new attraction will bring about world peace by bringing families closer together.

That's not what Cindy Gordon, vice president of new media and marketing partnerships at Universal Orlando Resort, did when she launched The Wizarding World of Harry Potter. Other large entertainment companies would have spent millions of dollars to interrupt everyone in the country with old-rules approaches: Super Bowl TV ads, blimps, direct mail, and magazine ads. Instead, Gordon told just seven people about the new attraction.

And those seven people told tens of thousands.

Then mainstream media listened to those tens of thousands and wrote about the news in their newspaper and magazine articles, in TV and radio reports, and in blog posts. Gordon estimates that 350 million people around the world heard the news that Universal Orlando

Resort was creating The Wizarding World of Harry Potter theme park.

Recognizing that millions of fans around the world are passionate about all things Harry Potter, Gordon knew she could rely on word-of-mouse to spread her story. After all, Harry is a global phenomenon. The series of books by author J.K. Rowling has been translated into sixty-five languages and has sold more than 325 million copies in more than 200 territories around the world. The films, produced by Warner Bros. Pictures, have grossed $3.5 billion worldwide at the box office.

Gordon and her counterpart at Warner Bros. chose to launch The Wizarding World of Harry Potter by first telling the exciting news to a very small group of rabid fans. Seven people at the top Harry Potter fan sites, such as Mugglenet, were hand-selected by Gordon's team, with Warner Bros. and Rowling herself providing input about the choices. These seven (affectionately referred to by Gordon's team as "the AP of the HP world") were invited to participate in a top-secret Webcast held at midnight on May 31, 2007.

The Webcast was hosted by Scott Trowbridge, vice president of Universal Creative, and featured Stuart Craig, the academy award-winning production designer for all the Harry Potter films. In the Webcast, live from the "Dumbledore's Office" set at Leavesden Studios, Craig discussed how his team of twenty designers is bringing together The Wizarding World of Harry Potter theme park.

"If we hadn't gone to fans first, there could have been a backlash," Gordon says. She imagined the disappointment dedicated Harry Potter fans might feel if they learned about Universal Orlando's plans in, say, The New York Times rather than an insider fan site.

Soon after the Webcast, the team sent an e-announcement to their in-house, opt-in e-mail list of park guests so they could hear the news directly too. Team members also sent the e-announcement to friends and family. During the secret Webcast, a Web micro-site went live to provide a place for bloggers and the media to link to for information on the *theme park, which is slated to open in late 2009 or early 2010. Visitors to the site learned that the park will feature immersive rides and interactive attractions, as well as experiential shops and restaurants that will enable guests to sample fare from the wizarding world's best known establishments.*

Because Gordon's team launched The Wizarding World of Harry Potter through social media—putting fans first—they were able to run the entire promotion in-house, with a very small marketing budget (covering the Webcast infrastructure and the micro-site production) and a tiny development team. They did not hire an agency, and they did no widespread outbound media relations, no marketing stunts, no CEO conference call, and no expensive advertising.

Of course, not all companies have Harry Potter on their team. But Gordon still accomplished a remarkable feat with an approach that most large organizations would not have taken. She told just seven people, and the power of word-of-mouse led to 350 million people hearing the news."

I know what you're thinking—that's Universal Studios, or Harry Potter, or Warner Brothers! Yes, they are all big brands with enough money to pay big bucks to market their products. Instead, they tapped into their raving fans and those fans became their online marketing force. The good news is *you can do the same thing.*

Content Marketing Builds Trust

This Cindy Gordon case study is a great example describing traditional push marketing methods in contrast to inbound marketing techniques which is what she used.

Push Marketing	Inbound Marketing
Super Bowl TV ads	Webcast
Blimps	E-announcement opt-in e-mail list
Direct mail	Web microsite
Magazine ads	Bloggers

As I've said before it's a mistake to use the social sites to do push marketing. Do you remember why? If not, revisit the section in chapter one on *Don't Be Salesy Pushy Slimy Sleazy*.

The bloggers at the top Harry Potter fan sites had a community with which they were sharing valuable and relevant content. Most likely, that content educated their community about Harry Potter and in doing so the bloggers built a relationship with their readers that helped them to know, like, and trust them. Cindy Gordon made a brilliant move when she decided to reach out to the bloggers at the top fan sites and leverage their relationships to communicate the message regarding the *Wizarding World of Harry Potter* to—yes, the world!

Content Marketing Informs Buyers

When you make a purchase for something you're not familiar with, how do you go about it? Do you run to the store? Do you watch an infomercial? Do you contact the sales rep? Many of us go online first. Why? Because we can take our time and hone in on exactly what we are looking for minus distractions, or pushy sales people, or being overwhelmed by an enormous amount of options.

In the purchase cycle, most of us do product research online first. Research suggests only 14 percent of us believe advertisements and commercials. Consequently, we go online for information minus commercials or advertisements. Instead, we look online at trusted sources to gather all the information to aid us in making an informed decision. During this process, we often check the opinions of trusted sources. It's very easy to go to our social sites where we are connected with friends and family and ask their opinions. Studies suggest 90% of us believe peer recommendations. So, if we are considering a purchase we are highly likely to ask our friends their opinions or refer to other trusted sources.

Think back to some of your purchases for technology and the process you used. Let me explain what I mean by telling you of a recent purchase.

A while back I had to replace the battery for my Dell XPS 15Z. Go figure! The battery is not covered under the warranty even though it is in the laptop! I went online to research batteries and replacement costs. Here's the pricing breakdown, which I thought was ridiculous!

1. $129 to have the battery replaced by a service technician
2. $159 for the cost of the battery itself

I'm no cheapskate; however, $388 seemed a bit much to replace a battery!

So, did I go to the Dell site first to get reviews and information on their battery? No! The first thing I did was go to YouTube to find out how to replace the battery. Sure enough, there was a video with step-by-step instructions, which alerted me to the fact there was no way it should cost $388 to have the battery replaced. Now I knew I could replace it myself.

Next, I did a Google search for the battery appropriate for my Dell model. I found battery options ranging in price from $29 to $399. I started to feel overwhelmed and uncertain. So I did a search on Dell batteries to get ideas from the support groups on the type of battery needed for my model.

I returned to the website where I found the batteries earlier and started reading the reviews; they helped me narrow down the options. I found the battery on sale. It was $145 on sale for $67 including a one-year warranty, and I could pay for it through PayPal, which made me feel safe. Consider this: I found lots of information from all these non-brand sources. As far as content marketing goes Dell has an excellent opportunity to serve their customers with valuable, relevant content on "How to choose a battery for your laptop"! It wouldn't hurt to educate people on how to replace the battery either.

This is my Dell after I installed the new battery. Scary, right?

Summary

Content marketing is important in creating presence and trust. Presence helps us get found by the people who are willing to pay for what we have to offer. The reality is we can only be in one place at a time, but content marketing gives us visibility—24 hours a day, seven days a week. It also opens doors to prospects we may not be able to reach otherwise. Content marketing is about sharing valuable, relevant content enabling prospects get to know, like, and trust us, with the ultimate end-goal of buying from us.

CHAPTER 3

The Fundamentals of Content Marketing and Social Media

I f you've ever seen me speak you probably heard the legend about the block of marble Michelangelo used to create the Statue of David.

Michelangelo had heard about a big block of marble eighteen feet high that was sitting around in a yard. He went to the town hall to ask about it and was told that the mayor had promised it to a sculptor called Sansovino. Another official said he had heard it was meant for Leonardo da Vinci. In any case, the best thing would be for Michelangelo to forget about it because it was worthless.

"Didn't they tell you?" said the official. "A fellow called Simone da Fiesole started to carve a statue years ago and the fool began by drilling a big hole right through the block. If it had been a clean hole maybe something could still be done; but then the guy goes and chips half the stone away from front and back of the hole too. A dozen sculptors have gone to look at it and they all come back here either angry or nearly crying. It was a beautiful block too, without any flaws. Da Fiesole ought to be hanged."

Michelangelo knew the story and he had often wondered just how bad the botch was and whether he couldn't cut a figure out of that block, hole and all. That a dozen other sculptors hadn't been able to do that didn't mean a thing to him. "Can I at least go and see it?" he asked.

In the yard of the Office of Works Michelangelo spent a long time at the stone. He walked around it, took measurements, stood in front of it in thought.

"Now you see for yourself why everyone else rejected the darn thing," said the old caretaker with all the keys; but he got no answer from Michelangelo.

As soon as he was home Michelangelo started drawing and making a little wax model of a David, which had been da Fiesole's subject. When he was sure he could carve his figure out of the botched block, he asked the mayor, Soderini, to give it to him.

He carved the David, according to Condivi, though few believe this, in eighteen months and "extracted the statue so exactly that the old rough surface of the marble [and da Fie-

sole's chisel marks] still appear on the top of the head and on the base."

There was a time when I thought content marketing was like that useless block of marble. Just like Michelangelo was told the marble was no good, you have likely been told that content marketing is no good and that it doesn't work.

My argument is this: if you did as Michelangelo did and strategized, created a plan, and worked the plan with committed, consistent effort you too could create a masterpiece just as Michelangelo did with the useless piece of stone.

"When all was finished, it cannot be denied that this work has carried off the palm from all other statues, modern or ancient, Greek or Latin; no other artwork is equal to it in any respect, with such just proportion, beauty and excellence did Michelangelo' finish it" **Giorgio Vasari**

Now that you know what content marketing is and why it's so important, the next logical question is: how do you get started? Here are seven steps you will need to take to create your content marketing masterpiece.

1. ***Create a content marketing strategy:*** In this step you identify your content's mission and objectives. You should also identify how you will set yourself apart and determine how you will measure your content marketing efforts. Your content is directed to your target market; therefore, you should craft your

buyer personas and research buyer persona pain points. All this enables you to create a content execution plan and a plan for repurposing the content.

2. *Pinpoint your keywords: This* is the key technical strategy for success with your content marketing. If you want your content to increase in exposure on search engines, you must create organic search credibility. Search credibility begins with knowing what keywords matter. Keyword research will lead you to find the keywords you *really* need to use versus what you *think* you should use.

3. *Prime to use hashtags:* Hashtags are used on many social sites. They are a way of organizing content so that it's searchable. They can be an effective branding tool, but just like keywords they need to be planned for and researched.

4. *Create an Editorial Calendar:* Content marketing can be a huge time and creativity vampire. By developing an editorial calendar, you will plan education-based marketing themes—themes around your sales, promotions, and events—as well as your hashtags and keywords that you can use throughout an entire year.

5. *Optimize your keyword titles and content:* The key to communication is reaching your prospect at an emotional level. Research shows there is "basic underlying harmonics, a tonality that flows through language, which are in many ways more profound and powerful than the dictionary meaning itself. Whereas sometimes meaning can be mistaken, the sound tones are always interpreted the same way by the emotions." By using the right keywords in your title, you can involve your reader in your content and invoke their deeper thoughts to entice them to read more.

6. ***Write using the Keep It Simple Success Model:*** To keep your reader engaged you will want to apply an acceptable readability score to your content. According to Grant Draper, a writer for *MarketingProfs*, "When someone is reading, the mind and eyes focus on 'successive points' allowing for a tentative judgment to be made in the mind of the reader as to what the text means up to that point. Natural breaks in the text, such as punctuation marks or new paragraphs, allow the mind to re-evaluate the text up to the point, when the mind stops for a split second, until it eventually arrives at the final meaning. The longer the word, sentence, or paragraph, the longer the brain has to suspend comprehending ideas until it can reach a point where all of the

words make sense together. Because they require more mental work by the reader, longer words and sentences are harder to read and understand."

7. *Publish valuable, relevant quality content*: Your content must respect the culture and language of the social sites. There is a universe of social media platforms available with a variety of capabilities. Some social networking sites are more appropriately suited to your business needs than others. Consequently, you should understand that each platform has unique features, unique culture, unique language, and unique tone. It is the platform's uniqueness that attracts its members. They are drawn to embrace the platform's cultural norms. To help you succeed with your content marketing, here are my thoughts on understanding the cultural norms and language of a few of the social networking sites:

- *Blogs*: Your goal is to dominate search engines. Blogging is really the secret sauce to social media success; consequently, it is a big part of your content marketing success—that and the little pink spoons I spoke of earlier. It is the non-salesy way for people to learn about you and your product or service. It is a smart and easy way to build credibility and trust. And, again, it is the *easiest* way to dominate search engines.

If you read blogs, you probably have an expectation of what you will get from the writer as far as topic and industry. For example, if you read a fashion blog you have an expectation around receiving fashion advice, tips about clothing, makeup, accessories, etc. If fashion bloggers started writing about auto repair, they would violate the culture and language of the community they created.

When blogging you write to speak to your target market or prospects providing them with valuable and relevant content that satisfies their pain points. I've always thought it is a good idea to choose a general topic area that leaves you room to grow. You don't want to get locked into such a narrow topic that could result in you running out of ideas. In my earlier example, fashion would be the general topic area leaving room for a multitude of topics without running out of ideas in the fashion genre.

- *YouTube:* Your goal is to be seen. According to their Advertising Department, "*YouTube* is the leader in online video, and the premier destination to watch and share original videos worldwide through a web experience. *YouTube* has 105 million unique users searching and discovering video on *YouTube* every month. That's why if you have video assets, *YouTube* is the logical place to expose them. Your *YouTube* Channel is your own 24/7 channel where your brand is the star! It's a place where you can build and engage a loyal audience of supporters directly on *YouTube*."

The culture of YouTube is like Times Square on New Year's Eve. It's crowded, loud and noisy. Your challenge is to find a way to stand out from the crowd to be seen by your target audience, *not* everyone on the Internet.

Meredith Levine writes about the types of videos that form the culture of YouTube in her blog *10 Videos to Watch to Understand the Culture of YouTube*. In a way, you can think of these as different languages spoken in the YouTube culture:

1. The Little Moments
2. The Big Moments
3. Fanvids
4. Cover Songs
5. How-to's/Tutorials/Instructional
6. Watching someone else play a video game

7. Comedy
8. International Content
9. Memes (a humorous image, video, a piece of text, etc. that is often copied with slight variations) and spread rapidly by Internet users.
10. Cuteness

- **Google Plus:** Your goal is to get found in the search engines. In my social media seminars, I ask participants if they wanted to use Google Plus when it came out. It turns out most people didn't want to—possibly because it wasn't Google's first attempt at creating and sustaining a social network. Actually, I think it may have been their third. Who wants to commit time to a social site that's not going to pan out? Many of my seminar participants say they still don't want to use Google Plus. However, like it or not, all things Google are good for SEO!

  Vishal Pindoriya describes G+ as "a 'social layer' consisting of not just a single site, but rather an overarching 'layer' which covers many of its online properties." He goes on to say that "Google+ *is* Google, Gmail, Maps, Chrome, Android, Ads, YouTube and more. With Google + instead of the assumption that everyone is your friend, you put everyone in appropriate groups called *circles.*"

The Google Plus culture is similar to a huge super shopping mall like Mall of America or The Dubai Mall. I remember talking with my friend Jennifer Buck, who says, "On G+, you have every walk of life, culture, religious and social belief system. While (you may not want to buy the goods) you still have a chance to look at it, touch it and, possibly, leave it right where it sits." In a mall, the stores would be equivalent to the circles and, of course, there are all kinds of store. The expectation when you go to a mall is to engage in a variety of ways with an absolute diversity of people, foods, shops, specialty stores and more. Well, that's the goal of Google Plus.

• **Twitter**: Your goal when using Twitter is to share what's going on in your business.

    The culture of Twitter is like a chamber cocktail party or trade show. Have you ever been to one of those events? If so, you've probably been overwhelmed by the pushy person using the event to sell you something. What a turn-off. That's not why we attend these events, and that's not why people are on Twitter. After you develop a relationship, sales naturally occur but if every tweet sells not only will you quickly lose followers you may even get reported as a spammer.

    People are on Twitter for:

1. Networking
2. Building Traffic
3. Business Promotion
4. Social Communication

Twitter is a challenge to understand for many people. Twitter is a microblogging platform. It "differs from a traditional blog in that its content is typically smaller in both actual and aggregate file size. Microblogs allow users to exchange small elements of content such as short sentences, individual images, or video links." Wikipedia

Twitter limits you to 140 characters making it tough to say something powerful, so the messages called *tweets* include URLs containing amazing content found in blogs, videos, images, SlideShare presentations, etc. In the big scheme of things, you'll want people to click on links and love your Tweets so much they share them (otherwise known as *retweets*) with others.

- *Facebook*: Your goal is to build a tribe of raving fans. The culture of Facebook is like a big family reunion picnic. In my family, we can only stand each other so much, so we have our family reunion picnic every 10 years. Imagine who comes:

o All the elders, of course, because they don't know if they will make through another 10 years.

o Out of town and local family members.

o Neighborhood friends.

o High school and college classmates.

o Let's not forget the exes—they come too. I don't know why, they just do.

At your family reunion picnic what activities do people participate in? There are games like football and basketball, board games like Monopoly and Chess or card games, people eat, drink, form cliques and gossip, reminisce, and share photos and videos. All these same things happen on Facebook.

If you were to go around selling your wares— vacuum cleaners, jewelry, candles, makeup, etc., at the family reunion picnic, what do you think would happen? People would avoid you. And that's exactly what happens on Facebook. They simply block you or unfriend you. While it's appropriate for your Facebook business page to market and sell your products and services, it's better to do so by tapping into the picnic culture using contests, sweepstakes, games, videos, photos, polls and stories.

• **LinkedIn**: Your goal is to expand and leverage your professional network. LinkedIn is the premier business networking site. Think of the culture like that of a corporate boardroom. In the same sense that YouTube has different languages within the culture so does LinkedIn. Here are some of the options:

1. Business Networking
2. Job Search
3. Thought Leadership
4. Business Marketing
5. Recruiting

Each of these options dictates a different communication style.

Summary

All social sites have a culture and language. Culture and language influence the content you will post. It's important to note that you don't need to be on every social site or the latest and greatest new site because your customers and prospects are not on all of them. In the beginning find out what social sites your target market is hanging out at and start your content marketing there. Before you start, you will need to develop a content marketing strategy. I'll show how to develop yours in the next chapter.

"Social media is not just an activity; it is an investment of valuable time and resources. Surround yourself with people who not just support you and stay with you, but inform your thinking about ways to WOW your online presence."
Sean Gardner

CHAPTER 4

Create a Content Marketing Strategy

A successful content strategy requires producing content that corresponds to the concerns and interest of your buyer personas. What is a buyer persona? The following definition from blog.hubspot.com sums it up nicely:

> "A **buyer persona** is a semi-fictional representation of your ideal customer based on market research and real data about your existing customers. When creating your **buyer persona(s)**, consider including customer demographics, behavior patterns, motivations, and goals. The more detailed you are, the better."

The content strategy focuses on creating buyer persona driven content that helps prospects get to know, like, and trust you. It's critical the content is compelling and that it delivers real value because relevant and valuable content creates leads that converts to customers. The content is not designed to pitch products or services. Instead, its purpose is to deliver information that makes the prospect more intelligent or that solves their day-to-day challenges.

> *"The purpose of content strategy is to facilitate the consistent delivery of interesting stories. The end result is that you will attract and retain the attention of the targeted audience that you want to reach."* Kristina Halvorson

Picture Your Target Market

Creating a picture of your target market will help you tailor your content to meet the needs of your buyer personas. There is a buyer persona tool developed by marketing strategist, Ardath Albee called *Up Close & Persona*™ . You can use it to craft your buyer personas. It steps you through answering all the necessary questions. The questions include:

- Defining or naming the industry your persona works in. *My industry is consulting.*
- Determining the average size of companies (number of employees) that you usually target. *The average size of my target market is 1 – 50 employees.*

- Determining your persona's annual revenue. *Typically, the companies I work with generate $100,000 - $500,000 in annual revenue.*
- Deciding if the typical company is bureaucratic or democratic. *My answer is democratic (or at least I hope so!).*
- Figuring out who or what can aid in or stall a buying decision. *In my case, limited time and money will absolutely stall a buying decision.*
- Determining the current trends. *I answered it this way: Social media is increasingly important for marketing, having a career or executive coach is the in thing for developing your business.*
- Identifying the industry leaders. *Mari Smith, Vivika von Rosen, Jon Loomer, and Amy Porterfield are all social media heavy-hitters.*
- Identifying new companies that may be gaining market share. *No doubt, Hootsuite, and Hubspot are contenders.*

As you can see, there is no need to sit there scratching your head trying to figure out your buyer persona. Use this excellent tool to help you figure it out!

Clues to Target Market Pain Points

Your target market gives you clues as to what their pain points are. Just think about your buyer persona and the types of questions they always ask about your product, industry or service. You should also think about the subject areas they bring up and the content platforms they go to for answers. Those clues are a great start in terms of creating content to respond to the pain points.

For example, in your line of work haven't you been asked the same question repeatedly? You've been asked the same questions so many times that someone broke down and put a list of frequently asked questions on your website. You know I'm right! If you doubt me, go to your website and look at the FAQs. Guess what? Each of those frequently asked questions came from your confused buyer personas (target market). Not just one but hundreds, so many, that your company employees got tired of answering those questions, so they put them on the company's website.

By the way, each frequently asked question could make a great blog post or question of the day on one of your social sites.

I don't think people look at the FAQs, do you? I can't say it's the first place I think of to find answers. My first stop is usually YouTube. Let me give you an example of what I mean. I have this portable hard drive that stopped working because of a bad connector. It's a common part, but the part was discontinued so I couldn't replace it with a simple Amazon order.

I knew the drive was still functional because I checked it earlier. I just needed a way to make it work. Apparently, I was not alone! Hundreds of thousands of PC users and owners have been in the same situation. Otherwise, I would not have been able to run over to *Best Buy* and purchase a new enclosure complete with a working connector.

I was ready to put my old drive in this new enclosure but discovered I had a new problem. I could not figure out how to get the drive out of the old case. It was time for YouTube™. I searched on "How to open a Seagate Freeagent Goflex case" and voila!—there were lots of videos, most of them not more than five minutes long. Tada! In minutes, I had a new working portable drive. Did I tell you the video was produced by some kid who sounded like Ted from *Bill & Ted's Excellent Adventure?* I'm just pointing out that it was not produced by Seagate!

I believe you have content suitable for your buyer personas because you've created it already. It's everywhere in your work environment as well as online in print and digital formats. Here is an activity to help you gather it.

The Company Content Marketing Scavenger Hunt

Wikipedia describes a scavenger hunt as *"a party game in which the organizers prepare a list defining specific items, which the participants – individuals or teams – seek to gather all items on the list – usually without purchasing them – or perform tasks or take photographs of the items, as specified. The goal is usually to be the first to complete the list, although in a variation on the game players can also be challenged to complete the tasks on the list in the most creative manner."*

Your assignment is to:

1. Get a few teams together at your workplace (make this a fun activity with prizes for the best team and the most unique finds.) You are going to have a content scavenger hunt. Although the purpose of the content is for your social sites, you should keep that to yourself to avoid people judging the content they find. It's more important to gather it than it is to judge it. The content is anything that has to do with your company, its people, products, and services.

2. Give your teams the following list and a day to find as many things on the list as possible. You should record the scavenger hunt, and at the end of the day get everyone together and have the groups do presentations of what they found. You should also record the presentations. This can make great content for your social sites, too.

Scavenger Hunt List

Your assignment is to find as much and as many of these types of items as possible. The first group to get them all wins a _____ (you decide). Your team has 24 hours.

1. White Papers
2. Research Papers
3. Guest-authored articles
4. Third-party Media Coverage
5. Videos
6. Photos

7. Testimonials
8. Case Studies
9. Webinars
10. Podcasts

11. Technical Manual
12. Marketing Brochures

13. Newsletters

14. News Stories
15. Historical records

16. Annual Reports
16. FAQs
17. Awards
18. Milestones

19. Press Releases
20. PowerPoint Presentations
21. Art
22. State of the business
23. Recipes
24. Quotes from founders and leaders of the company
25. Infographics and other non-written forms of content
26. Behind the scenes photos: Work in progress; event preparation, etc.

Do the Jedi Mind Trick to
Your Target Market

As a Star Wars fan, I'd like to suggest you learn the Jedi Mind trick for the purpose of gathering content from employees and customers. Mark Memmott says, "Jedi knights, from Star Wars, are of course known for their mind tricks: a spectrum of Force powers which influenced the thoughts of sentient creatures, most commonly used to coerce into agreement by suggestion through voice manipulation, or to cause one to reveal information." In other words, you have to influence your customers and employees to give you content. Allow me to explain.

There are years of content in the heads of your employees and customers, so find ways to get it out. You can do so by conducting interviews, surveys, or soliciting testimonials—these are just a few examples. You have tons of content that you will want to collect during company's sales, promotions, and charity events. Collect it! Start capturing it in pictures and videos. Turn the switch on in your head that looks for candid camera type moments and *America's Funniest Home Video* type moments.

Are you familiar with *America's Funniest Home Videos?*

"Hosted by Emmy Award winner Tom Bergeron, America's Funniest Home Videos is the longest-running primetime entertainment show in the history of ABC. Each week, the AFV team evaluates thousands of user-submitted home vid-

eos, to bring you America's 'real-life' funny moments captured on video.

AFV offers a weekly $10,000 first place prize to the funniest or most unusual video as voted upon by the in-studio audience. Those prize winners then move on to the next competition round where they vie for a $100,000 prize. At the end of the season, the $100,000 prize winners compete for a Grand Prize vacation package. In its 24 seasons to date, AFV has given away over $13 million in prize money and evaluated more than a million videotapes from home viewers.

AFV has become an iconic part of American pop culture, as evidenced by its entry into the Smithsonian's permanent entertainment collection. Today, AFV is syndicated in over 50 countries around the world, spreading American humor and clumsiness across the globe!"

Again, I explained AFV to help you understand how those special moments that happen in your business can translate into valuable content. Other ideas you might want to consider include doing special interest stories on your processes, projects, and employees. For instance, how they give back to the community or feature a customer of the week or month.

A Content Marketing Themes Mind Map

A mind map can help you get additional content ideas out as well as organize the content you've gathered during the scavenger hunt.

Think of mind mapping as a way to outline your ideas in a visual manner. Keep in mind that not every idea will be an idea that you use; however, just getting your ideas out will spark creative ways to reach your target audience.

"A mind map is a diagram used to visually organize infor-mation. A mind map is often created around a single con-cept, drawn as an image in the center of a blank landscape page, to which associated representations of ideas such as images, words and parts of words are added." Wikipedia

Here are five steps to help you create a Mindmap. I cre-ated the steps in Microsoft Word to give you a visual. There are several different free programs available to create your mind map, namely, *Freeplane, Freemind, XMind, Coggle, MindJet, Mindnode, Scrapple, and Mind Meister.* I'm sure there are more, but these are the ones that people use the most.

1. You will need a center element. In this example, I've used "Social Media Content Themes" as my center ele-ment.

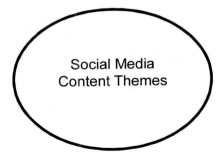

2. Look at your mind map and decide on sub-topics that fit or are a natural outflow of your central theme.

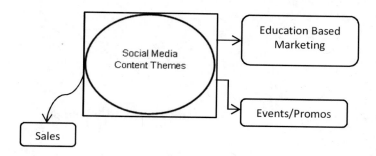

3. It's time to drill down and create information related to each subtopic.

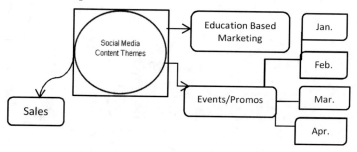

4. As you continue to drill down, in step four you will begin to uncover your keywords:

5. In step five you will begin to notice topics that fit well
    with your sub-topics.

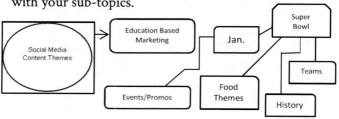

Part of your content strategy could include brainstorm-
ing education-based marketing themes. You also might
want to consider creating content based on your sales,
promotions, and events. Again, when you brainstorm to do
your mind map, forget about your company and just focus
on getting ideas out.

Summary

In part one, you plan your content marketing strategy.
During planning, identify what social sites you will post
your content to. I will make recommendations later. Just
keep in mind you are selecting the site where your buyer
personas are most likely spending time.

Many of my clients instantly stress at the idea of creating
content. They imagine it takes hours upon hours of work.
The reality is there is valuable, relevant content all around
you. If you are too judgmental, you might not notice it, or
possibly you didn't think the content would be suitable for
your social sites. Now that you know about the culture and

language of the sites my hope is you have a more open per-spective on how to use the variety of content I'm sure you have.

Now that you have an idea of what content you might use, in part two, I will show you how to identify the key-words to include in your content.

"You cannot go wrong by investing in communities and the human beings within them."
Pam Moore

CHAPTER 5

The Insider Steps to Identify Powerful Keywords

I n this chapter I want to explain the concept and the importance of keywords. Let's first start with a definition.

> "Keywords are single words, or more commonly strings of words, that represent the content of a web page and how people ask for web content. Keywords are strategically selected by optimizers and are intended to help your web content communicate in a way that resonates with humans and Google search spiders." Chelsea Adams

Keywords define what your page and its content are about. You will incorporate the keywords both in the body of your text and in the headings and subheadings in a subtle, yet natural way. When done well, your reader can easily digest the keyword phrases along with the rest of the content.

If you want to go to Google jail (I think I just made that up), then use keywords to trick and mislead readers and Google spiders. This is accomplished by using keywords that do not exactly describe the content of your page, and repeating a keyword over and over in a way that is not natural. This is called keyword stuffing.

Who Cares About Keywords?

If you're still wondering who cares about keywords, this should answer the question. When people have problems, they often go on the Internet searching for the problem— not necessarily the solution to the problem. Although I often start a search with the words "how to . . . ," I believe that while your brand may be able to fix the problem if your potential customers don't know you exist they won't know to look for your company, product or service. By including keywords and phrases in your content, you are leaving breadcrumbs that lead people with a problem to your product or service that can help them solve that problem. Consider the following example.

I pretty much popped out from the womb needing to wear glasses. I always hated having them touch my face. Not to mention how they would fall off and get bent out of shape. About 15 years ago I had Lasik surgery. As soon as the surgery was complete I could see the microscopic organisms in the air. Okay that might be a slight exaggeration, but it is no exaggeration to say my eyesight improved immediately and drastically. No more glasses or contacts! Hurray!

I thought the surgery's impact would last forever. However, now I'm noticing I can see the words on a sign across the street, but I cannot see the words on the paper I'm holding in my hand. So imagine that I go to Google to search for a solution to this problem. What do you suppose the search argument would be? "Where do I get eyeglasses?" or "Where do I get contact lenses?" These are both solutions to the problem. Remember, I believe more often than not people look at the problem and not the solution. Consequently, the search argument might be "why can't I see up close?" The typical search results included a blog post pretty much telling me that I'm at the age where I will have to where glass again if I want to see up close. Really?

How to Identify Your Keywords

It is important that you start thinking like your buyer personas, your customers, and your target market. Make a broad list of keyword and keyword phrases they would use when they have problems that your product or service would correct or resolve.

Remember to think like a potential customer who doesn't know your business exists. All they know is that they have a certain problem or need, and they are searching to find someone who offers the solution through a product or service. Furthermore, remember that people are smart about searching for what they want; consequently, they are going to search on a targeted phrase. For instance, in my example above the search results gave me the impression that I may need glasses or contacts if I want to see up close. I'm not excited by either of these propositions. I wanted another option. Back at Google search central (ha ha) do you suppose I would do a search on "eye"? Not likely. How about "I don't want to wear eyeglasses or contacts any-more—alternatives."

Are These Really Keywords?

Just because you *think* your customers use certain keywords or phrases doesn't make it true. To find out for sure, you should use tools like Google Keyword Planner or other free keyword tools. The Google Keyword Planner has an entire suite of features that will help you identify if a keyword is growing (or shrinking) in popularity. It will also help you filter out low-volume searches and create hundreds of key-word combinations in seconds. There are many guides and how to's available on the Internet that show you how to use the Google Keyword Planner. Keep in mind I'm suggesting you use the tool to identify keywords for your content mar-keting. The tool is designed for a company that wants to do paid advertising on Google. Most of the information you find is directed to them. Nevertheless, the tool is free and worth checking out. There are many other keyword tools. So if you don't like Google's tool, you can try some of the others.

Topsy is another tool you can use to conduct research for the best keywords and keyword phrases. My Topsy research yielded the popularity of three keyword phrases: content marketing, education-based marketing, and social media marketing during the month of January.

Note that every time you create long-form content (this is your lengthier content such as blog posts typically longer than 900 words) you will conduct keyword research. The research is critical so you know what keywords to include in the content you create. Now that we've discussed keyword research let's proceed to part three: planning for hashtags.

Summary

When Internet users are looking for a specific item such as product or service, or if they have a specific kind of problem, they input keywords and phrases into search engines to be led to a solution. You will want to use the keywords and phrases in your content marketing that your target market uses so that you get found. In other words, don't guess the keywords; use tools to help you identify them.

"Nobody reads ads. People read what interests them. Sometimes, it's an ad." Howard Gossage

CHAPTER 6

How to Improve Content Marketing With Edgy Hashtags

S o you're wondering *what* is a hashtag, right? A hashtag is a set of characters used to organize content in social media. It's a word or phrase prepended by (#) and is followed by some characters; here is an example #socialmediastrategist. Here's a bit of trivia according to *The Do's and Don'ts of How to Use Hashtags*: "The hashtag is so recognized that it was added to the Oxford dictionary in 2010, and the Scrabble Dictionary in 2015 (#standards)."

Using a hashtag makes the content searchable if that content contains that unique acronym or phrase. Think of hashtags as putting a label on a file folder. In this example, the label is the hashtag, and the content in the file folder is related to the hashtag. When you see hashtags on social sites just click on them and you can see all the conversations taking place around that particular hashtag. They are also searchable on Google.

Here is an example. Often when I share educational content about social media, I include the hashtag #socialmediastrategist. A Facebook search of the hashtag returns lots of results. Go ahead and search Facebook on that hashtag to get an idea of the volumes of results you'll receive from just one hashtag.

A Twitter search of the hashtag returns lots of results too. Take a minute to do a Twitter search for #socialmediastrategist to see what I mean.

Even a Google search will return lots of unique results. As with Facebook and Twitter, do a hashtag search on Google to compare the differences.

Now, put your marketing hat on. Wouldn't it be awesome for your customer who searched on your niche hashtags to find valuable, relevant content that informs them about your products, services or brand?

Hashtags have gained widespread acceptance and are used on numerous social sites, including Twitter, Facebook, Google+, Instagram, Vine and Pinterest. And even though it's no longer searchable on LinkedIn, I continue to use it there in hopes that it will be searched elsewhere. Hashtags give your content visibility by anyone with an interest in your hashtag. Plan the right hashtags for your content and make sure you're using the right number of hashtags in your content.

Planning for Hashtags

Hashtag rules dictate that you use no more than three hashtags in your content. You may want to conduct hashtag research before deciding on hashtags to use. This will ensure the hashtag is not being used in a way your brand doesn't want to be associated.

For example, I was doing hashtag research for South Coast Air Quality Management District (SCAQMD). Their company tagline is "Cleaning the Air That We Breath." I love it, but #CleaningtheAirThatWeBreath, in my opinion, is too long. The problem with lengthy hashtags is that people won't use them. The brand will, but your goal is to get your friends, fans and followers to use them as well. You have to make it easy! Remember, people don't want to type that many letters.

What are some other options? I cleverly thought of #AWB (Air We Breathe), and until I did the research, I had completely forgotten about the *Average White Band* and just learned about *Artist Without Borders*. Oh yeah, there are also *Astronauts Without Borders*; who knew? This just goes to show that although these are popular hashtags, I don't think SCAQMD would want to be associated with them.

You want people to naturally search for your tag. Hashtags are supposed to make your brand easier to find and easier to engage. In this case, you're better off with something like #cleantheair or #cleanair. Hashtag research shows there are a lot of conversations going on with both of them, and the conversations are relevant to what SCQAMD is all about.

There are many sources for doing hashtag research. Here are just a few:

- https://www.hashtags.org is a great place to start. You will get essential information, research, and how-to knowledge to help you improve your social media branding and social media intelligence. You will also find articles organized into an online guide entitled *Quick Start to Hashtags*. The articles are categorized as follows (according to their website):

  o *Background* information on hashtags used by Twitter, Google Plus, and many other social media sites.
  o *Etiquette* to prevent you from making a social media faux pas.
  o *History* to include how hashtags came to exist in 2007 and how they are used on various social media networks.

- o *Marketing* instructions to teach you how to use Twitter and other tools to boost your marketing strategies.
- o *Search* guide that will help you to find things and get found.
- o *Tips* to provide you with the assistance you will need to ensure you're moving in the right direction. As they say on the site, "This section goes beyond hashtags to help you start and thrive."
- o *Social Networks* gives you guidance and direction on the various social networking platforms.

- https://ritetag.com According to their website, Ritetag "streamlines the process of finding the best tags to go with content to be shared, embracing the unique tagging constraints of numerous important content-sharing networks." They argue "well-chosen hashtags greatly increase discovery by searchers, tag-trackers, and hashtag clickers. Which hashtags get the outcomes you need, though? RiteTag identifies hashtags that got results and leads you to use them more, continually refining your smart-tagging."

- https://www.hashatit.com *Hash At It* claims to be the first Social Search Engine for hashtags (#). You can search hashtags on today's most popular social networks: Facebook, Twitter, Instagram, and Pinterest. They give you a quick and easy way to sort through hashtags, bringing all conversations to one place in real time.

* http://keyhole.co Track hashtags, keywords and URLs in real-time. Keyhole's hashtag analytics dashboard is comprehensive, beautiful and shareable! At their About Page they say:

"We believe that paying attention to your audience, and reaching out to people who are relevant, should be easy. Unfortunately, it's not.

We've all had to track Twitter conversations in the past, opened up a Search column only to be overwhelmed, and then thought: "There has to be a better way than this!"

Same here.

First, we created a solution for ourselves internally. The response was so great - as much for the format as the data -- that we realized we're not the only ones who would find this valuable. The big guys may have heavy duty (and super-expensive) tools, but there are other small companies out there like us. So we made it into its own product, which is what you're seeing here.

From solving our pain point to hopefully solving yours— Hope it helps, and let us know if you have any feedback."

Hashtag Marketing Strategies

When deciding on hashtags remember why they are so powerful. Be strategic when choosing them and look for ways to connect your brand with various popular and incredibly visible topics. This will drive new viewers to your social media presence and give you the opportunity to engage with them. Well-crafted, sparingly used hashtags can help increase your visibility and even improve customer relations.

Here is another SCAQMD example: SCAQMD has this big event every year called *The Lawn Mower Exchange*. While they did tweet about it and even included a hyperlink to Facebook, they failed to use hashtags. When I clicked on the hyperlink in the tweet, it took me to their Facebook Page where I saw a flyer for the event—still, no hashtag on the flyer either. That's great real estate for hashtags. Interestingly enough, they did include #TradeMyMower in their Facebook post. Here's my point: Not only do you want to use hashtags consistently across all your social media networks, you will also want to include them on your printed marketing brochures and advertisements.

More Hashtag Marketing Strategies

Here are three additional hashtag marketing strategies that you should also consider when crafting and using hashtags:

- *Brand specific:* These are hashtags that you make for your own business. Use them to market your brand and promotions. It might be your company name or a company tagline. A brand hashtag is unique to your business and defines your business. Use it as your signature tag to get people to use them so that your brand gets marketed too. You want it to be short and easy to spell. Here's my example: #Iamasocialmediatrainer is too long, and #socialmediastrategist is better.

- *Campaign specific:* This is the place to use the name of your current marketing campaign. Pick a word or phrase that is unique to your short-term contest or promotion. Avoid using really popular hashtags. In fact, I suggest you follow the advice of bigwishpond.com:

"Promote your campaign hashtags as a method for your customers to engage with you and your other customers throughout the duration of your special offer. For example,

include the use of your hashtag as a requirement to enter your contest."

In the example of SCAQMD's lawn mower exchange, their campaign hashtag appears to be #TradeMyMower. It needs to be included in all social posts and printed collateral pertaining to the event.

- *Content specific:* Hashtags are used in your posts to improve the SEO. In the section covering keywords, you should now understand that keywords contribute to search engine optimization (SEO). Consumers who are searching for, or using the hashtag words will see your updates. Try these hashtags categories:

    - Product = #pumpkinspicelatte
    - Lifestyle = #cleaneating
    - Event = #ballonfestival
    - Location = #grandcanyon

Summary

By now you know that a hashtag is a set of characters used to organize content in social media. Using a hashtag makes the content searchable if that content contains that unique acronym or phrase. You will want to use hashtags so when your customer searches on your niche hashtag they will find valuable, relevant content that informs them about your products, services or brand. Hashtags are used on numerous social sites including Twitter, Facebook, Google+, Instagram, Vine, and Pinterest. Before using hashtags conduct research to make an informed choice and apply the three hashtag marketing strategies outlined in this chapter.

Now that you have your keywords, hashtags and topic themes, you can lay it all out on an editorial calendar.

CHAPTER 7

Creating a Practical and Powerful Editorial Calendar for the Year

The one-man band like many small-business owners and entrepreneurs, pulled in all directions, has limited time and money to spend on marketing, social media or content marketing. So it's critical to participate on social platforms that give you the biggest return for your time and your efforts. In other words, you will need to practice good time management.

Good time management means participating on the right social platforms. Your decisions must be made based on your target market, platforms they use, Google page rank, and SEO advantage. Given these considerations, you will not only blog, but you will likely use the major social sites such as Facebook, Twitter, LinkedIn, YouTube, Google+, and Pinterest. Good time management also means you plan in advance what your content themes, keywords, and hashtags will be for all your social sites. That is where the editorial calendar comes in.

Your editorial calendar is a listing of your planned content including the themes and hashtags you intend to use in your content marketing. There are many templates online for editorial calendars. Some are quite elaborate. However, this process doesn't have to be complicated. It can be as simple as pulling up your Outlook or Gmail Calendar and using it to list your content themes and hashtags once you've planned them using this template.

Social Media Editorial Calendar

Facebook			
	Little Pink Spoons	Keywords	Hashtags
Theme 1			
Theme 2			
Theme 3			
Theme 4			
Twitter			
Theme 1			
Theme 2			
Theme 3			
Theme 4			

LinkedIn			
Theme 1			
Theme 2			
Theme 3			
Theme 4			
Blog			
Theme 1			
Theme 2			
Theme 3			
Theme 4			
Google+			
Theme 1			
Theme 2			
Theme 3			
Theme 4			
YouTube			
Theme 1			
Theme 2			
Theme 3			
Theme 4			
Pinterest			
Theme 1			
Theme 2			
Theme 3			
Theme 4			

Why Use an Editorial Calendar

Most people would agree that social media can be a time vampire. I remember when I first started using social media I planned to spend just 30 minutes twice a day doing social media marketing. I would start with Facebooks at 6:30 a.m. I had the best of intentions to move through as many of my social sites as I could in the first 30 minutes and pick up where I left off in the last 30 minutes. Next thing I knew, I would look up and it would be 6:30 p.m. and I'd been Facebooking all day. Being a small-business owner I have tons of other things to do and Facebooking all day is not a good use of my time. It's probably not a good use of your time either.

The way to prevent the drain on your time is to have a system. I learned a long time ago as a trainer that systems create behaviors and those behaviors become automatic responses during a crisis like when you're sick, or had a sleepless night. They work amazingly well when you've had to fly all night, or get jarred awake at 3 a.m. by a fire alarm, or when you have to drive through a blizzard through the night to be able to deliver training the next morning.

Your editorial calendar is part of your social media system. It will save you time and energy. I poll my social media seminar participants regularly to find out how many blog. Only a few do. Those who don't blog are creating little pink spoons of content, running out of ideas, getting tired and end up posting content that is not branded, inconsistent with the company goals, or irrelevant to the brand goals. That's exhausting.

An editorial calendar will supply you with weeks and even months of content themes, keywords, and hashtags that you can leverage to create content that carries you through the year. The editorial calendar is a major time-saver. However, it does take time and effort to create.

How to use an Editorial Calendar

Go back to your mind map and select appropriate content themes for your brand. For example, in chapter four when we did the mind map if we had drilled down even further, we could have brainstormed Super Bowl food themes. We would have uncovered food themes suitable for all kinds of businesses. Can you think of a few? Here is a list of viable possibilities:

- Restaurants
- Hotels
- Bars
- Food trucks
- Natural medicine practitioners
- Health food stores
- Farmers Markets
- Grocery stores

- Bed and Breakfasts
- Ice cream shops

Suppose Whole Foods Market is planning to blog about Super Bowl food themes the entire week leading up to Super Bowl Sunday. There are more than enough topics under Super Bowl food themes to carry them through the week. See Appendix A for a larger example.

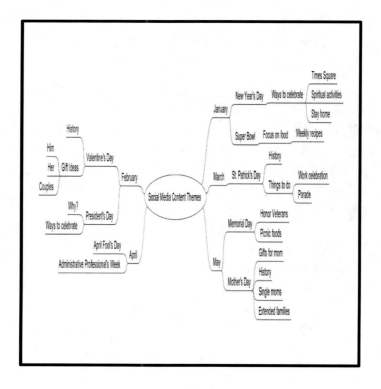

In the sample editorial calendar for February 2015, the themes selected are for a health clinic. The health clinic selected one keyword optimized theme (based on the keyword research) for every week of the month and popular hashtags. After selecting the themes, the next step is to craft content for the social sites. You have many options. One option is to go back to all the content you gathered from the scavenger hunt and find content that corresponds with your themes.

Also, think about your promotions and events. For example, suppose you have a product that you sell heavily during the holidays. You will want to start planning and strategizing your content marketing three to six months in advance. Then you will list on your editorial calendar the kinds of blogs you need to write about and post, as well as the other content that you will need, etc. All of that is going to help you be more successful if you use the editorial calendar to plan it.

The next decision is to determine what type of content to create. Will you just create blog content? Or will you leverage your blog content and repurpose it to make YouTube videos, pictures, infographics, status updates, tweets, etc.?

Also, remember your blog is the foundation of all your social media work. You spend time on the social media sites where your target market hangs out to build your relationships and a following to consume your content.

Study this simple editorial calendar on the following page and you will see that every week there are a couple of themes. The foundation of the content, in this case, is always built on keywords such as health, healthy living, and healthy since it is an editorial calendar for a health clinic. Note that each week has a different twist on health topics like the Super Bowl, Black History, Valentine's Day, and parties. Also note the hashtag options for every day. Don't forget you can find much more elaborate editorial calendars, but it can be as simple as this.

February 2015

	February 2015							March 2015					
Su	Mo	Tu	We	Th	Fr	Sa	Su	Mo	Tu	We	Th	Fr	Sa
1	2	3	4	5	6	7	1	2	3	4	5	6	7
8	9	10	11	12	13	14	8	9	10	11	12	13	14
15	16	17	18	19	20	21	15	16	17	18	19	20	21
22	23	24	25	26	27	28	22	23	24	25	26	27	28
							29	30	31				

SUNDAY	MONDAY	TUESDAY	WEDNESDAY	THURSDAY	FRIDAY	SATURDAY
Feb 1 Superbowl health #SuperBowl #DomesticViolence #healthyliving	**2** Tips For Staying Healthy on Super Bowl Sunday #SuperBowl #DomesticViolence #healthyliving	**3** How to Stay Healthy During & After a Super Bowl Party #SuperBowl #DomesticViolence #healthyliving	**4** Survive the Super Bowl Health Tips and Recipes #SuperBowl #DomesticViolence #healthyliving	**5** Healthy superbowl gadgets #SuperBowl #DomesticViolence #healthyliving	**6** (Mostly) Healthy Superbowl Snacks healthy #SuperBowl #DomesticViolence #healthyliving	**7** Superbowl is over Be My Healthy Valentine! #medicine #CancerPrevention #heartattack #Diabetes #stress #HelpYourHeart
8 Healthy valentine's day recipes #medicine #CancerPrevention #heartattack #Diabetes #stress #HelpYourHeart #health	**9** Healthy valentine's day gifts #medicine #CancerPrevention #heartattack #Diabetes #stress #HelpYourHeart #health	**10** Healthy valentine's day ideas #medicine #CancerPrevention #heartattack #Diabetes #stress #HelpYourHeart #health	**11** Healthy valentine's day treats adults #medicine #CancerPrevention #heartattack #Diabetes #stress #HelpYourHeart	**12** Heart-Healthy Valentine's Day Tips #CancerPrevention #heartattack #Diabetes #stress #HelpYourHeart #health	**13** Healthy Valentine's Day breakfast in bed recipes. #medicine #CancerPrevention #heartattack #Diabetes #stress #HelpYourHeart	**14** Healthy valentine's day dinner. #medicine #CancerPrevention #heartattack #Diabetes #stress #HelpYourHeart #health
15 Healthy (and Fun) Mardi Gras Ideas #MardiGras #grammys #Cancersurvivors	**16** Healthy Mardi Gras Recipes and Menus #HelpYourHeart #health #MardiGras	**17** Fat Tuesday Eating Traditions and What They Mean for Your #CancerPrevention #heartattack #Diabetes #stress #HelpYourHeart	**18** Healthy Mardi Gras - Recipes for a Not So Fat Tuesday #CancerPrevention #heartattack #Diabetes #stress #HelpYourHeart	**19** 10 Healthy Ways to Celebrate Fat Tuesday #CancerPrevention #heartattack #Diabetes #stress #HelpYourHeart #health #MardiGras	**20** 2015 Grammy Awards focus on Domestic Violence Issue 2015 #grammys #CancerPrevention #heartattack #Diabetes #stress	**21** From Cancer survivor to Oscar Host Robin Roberts #CancerPrevention #heartattack #Diabetes #stress #HelpYourHeart
22 Black History Month health #BlackLivesMatter #blackhistorymonth #BHM2015 #medicine	**23** Black history month healthcare #BlackLivesMatter #blackhistorymonth #BHM2015 #medicine	**24** Black History Month - Salute to Health Care Heroes #BlackLivesMatter #blackhistorymonth #BHM2015 #medicine	**25** Honoring Black Medical Pioneers for Black History Month #BlackLivesMatter #blackhistorymonth #BHM2015 #medicine	**26** Black history healthcare facts #BlackLivesMatter #blackhistorymonth #BHM2015 #medicine	**27** Black history mental health #BlackLivesMatter #blackhistorymonth #BHM2015 #medicine	**28** Celebrating Black History Month with Wellness #BlackLivesMatter #blackhistorymonth #BHM2015 #medicine

Summary

The goal of your social media activity is to lead your fans to your blog—not your website or sales landing page but to your blog. The reason why is because your blog is the foundation of your social media activity. You will use your blog to educate your target market by sharing your wisdom, knowledge, expertise, and your products and services in a non-salesy slimy sleazy way—in other words, your blog is the tool for education-based marketing (EBM). You drive people to your blog in an education-based way where they learn more details, see the freebies you give away and get a sense of who you are in a more meaningful way.

The blog will help you convert people. From the blog, the goal is to get your fans to opt-in to your newsletter because part of social media is to capture the data so that you can continue to outbound market and not just strictly inbound market. Research shows that when you are able to capture that data and get them to opt-in to your newsletter you'll experience a 50% increase in your sales.

Once you get them to opt-in to your newsletter, you want your newsletter to feedback to your blog. If you are thinking OMG! This sounds like a lot of work—it just takes a system. Use the newsletter to tease them with what's in the blog (which is hosted on your website—FYI, blog content hosted on your website increases click-through rates). Research shows that first-time visitors to a website without a blog spend 12 seconds there before leaving. Contrast this with the fact that first-time visitors to a website with a blog spend 2 minutes and 30 seconds before leaving. That's a huge difference and will increase the likelihood of click-through rates to other pages on the site.

Share links to your blog and little pink spoons from your blog content on your social sites. For example, take the picture that was part of your blog content and post it on your Facebook page. Include the URL to your blog and a call to action that gets people to click on the link. Tease your Twitter followers with a different little pink spoon from the blog content. Include a link driving them back to your blog; also, ask them to retweet your content so that it spreads. From there move to your other social sites to share little enticing pink spoons of goodness from your blog content.

"The best marketing doesn't feel like marketing."
Tom Fishburne

CHAPTER 8

The Simple Truth about How to Keyword Optimize Your Titles and Content

This is the point where you take the keywords you researched and start using them to get found in search results. The first place you start is with the title of your content. There are a few reasons for keyword optimizing your titles.

The first reason is for your readers. Aren't you super busy? So are your readers. That means they don't have time to dig through your content to see if it really addresses their needs. Consequently, they skim your titles, headings and subheadings looking for clues trying to quickly decide if they should read further.

The second reason is search engines put more weight on the early words in titles such as your blog title. You will want your keywords near the beginning of the title because you are more likely to rank well. Here is an example to illustrate. Let's say the health clinic (from the last chapter) is trying to rank for the keywords "Healthy Eating," which title do you think would be best according to what's been said so far: "Black History Month Recipes for Healthy Eating" or "Healthy Eating Recipes for Celebrating Black History"? If you picked the second title, you are correct!

Another reason for putting your keywords at the beginning of your titles is because people looking at your content will scan search result pages and see the early words first. When your keywords are at the beginning of your content, it's more likely to get clicked on. Not to mention Google shows the first 60 to 70 characters of your title in the search results. In the next chapter, we will address the body of your content in more depth but as far as SEO goes, I also want you to know that it's important to include your keywords within the first 100 words of your content.

By now, you understand that titles are important to capture your reader's attention. Good titles evoke an emotional response, ask a question, or promise something (that the content fulfills). There is a formula, so to speak, for creating titles and headings; you'll learn more about that in the next section.

Creating Marketing Content T.I.T.L.E.S.

Now it's time to apply the keywords you researched. Optimize your content heading by including the keywords or keyword phrases you are trying to target at the beginning as discussed. Additionally, use keywords to send a strong message about the subject of your content. This helps your reader determine whether to keep reading or not. Your reader is going to scan your document for:

- Headings
- Subheadings
- Beginning of paragraphs
- Highlighted text
- Bullet Lists
- Number Lists

This list can serve as a formula for formatting your long-form content to improve readability. In each of these areas listed, lead with keywords or keyword phrases. To avoid getting into trouble with the search engines do not keyword stuff. Instead, use two to three keywords or keyword phrases for every 300 words of content. The following table uses the TITLES acronym for different types of titles you can create. A special thanks to Adam Vavrek, Director of Marketing Operations for Skyword for sharing this incredible formula with me and allowing me to share it with you.

TITLES	Emotionally Charged Words That Get a Reaction
Teasers	Which? Who? How? Should? Why? (Video, Photo, Poll, Infographic) Mistakes, New
Instructions	How to, Easy, Description, Steps, Ways
Threats	Warning, Alert, Caution, Look out for, Safe, Safety, Trust, Lies, Hoax, Money, Life, Actually, Concerns, Recall
Lists	The Top, Guide, Tips, Ways, Benefits, Signs
Engagement	You, Controversy, Debate, Surprising, Alarming
Secrets	Secret, Secrets, Just Like, Now, New, Simplify, Shortcut, Cheat Sheet

I've also included a long list of other types of titles I've compiled from my research.

Content Marketing Titles Templates

[#] Tips For _____
[#] Smart Strategies To _____
[#] Most Effective Tactics To _____
[#] Most Popular Ways To _____
[#] Essential Steps To _____
[#] Wrong Ways To_____
[#] Creative Ways _____
[#] Tips For Busy _____

[#] No-Nonsense ____
[#] Surprising ____
[#] Handy Tips From ____ For ____
[#] Superb Ways To ____ Without
[#] Tricks ____
[#] Ways To Make Sure Your ____ Is Not ____
[#] Mistakes You'll Never Make Again
[#] Mistakes You Don't Want To Make
[#] Tactics To ____
[#] Super Tips ____
[#] That Will Make You ____
[#] Foolproof ____ Tips For ____
[#] Epic Formula To ____
[#] Supercharge Your ____
[#] Pleasant Ways To ____
[#] Insane Ways To ____
[#] Unique Ways To ____
[#] Greatest ____ Hacks For ____
[#] Things You Didn't Know About ____
[#] Wittiest ____ To ____
[#] Manly Things To ____
[#] Outrageous ____
[#] Weird But Effective ____ For
[#] Things You Should Never Do ____
[#] Wearable ____ For ____
[#] Kick-Ass Ways To ____Like A Ninja!

How to

How To _____ That Drives _____

How To _____ in [#] easy steps

How To _____ in

How I Made _____ in _____

How To Find _____

How To Rock _____

How To Make A Strong _____

How To Completely Change _____

How To Create _____ That Gets _____

How To Get More _____

How To Generate More _____

How To Quickly _____

How To Deliver

How To Use _____ To Stand Out

How To Tell If _____

How _____ Boost Your _____

How To _____ The Right Way

How _____ Can Inspire Your _____

How To Get Rid Of _____

What To Do With _____

Where To Find _____

Quick Guide:

A Complete Guide To _____

What to Look for _____

Ultimate Guide: _____

Advanced Guide: _____

Beginners Guide: ____
Hack: ____
DIY ____
Practical Guide: ____
The Anatomy Of ____ That Gets ____
Full Guide: ____
How To Unlock ____
Getting Smart With

List Titles

[#] Things your ____ Doesn't Tell You
[#] ____ Trends For [YEAR]
[#] ____Every ____ Should Own
[#] ____ to Consider For ____
[#] Amazing ____ To Try Right Now
[#] Insane ____ That Will Give You ____
[#] Types of ____
[#] Questions You Should Ask Before ____
[#] Worth-It ____ For ____
[#] Jobs That Will Make You ____
[#] Secrets To ____
[#] Resources to Help You Become ____
[#] Ways to Embrace ____
[#] Proven Ways To ____
[#] Signs You Might ____
[#] Point Checklist: ____
[#] Pointers ____

[#] Rules For _____
[#] Habits Of _____
[#] Things You Need To Know Before _____
[#] Ideas To _____
[#] Trends You Need To Know _____
[#] Best _____ To _____
[#] _____ We Love
[#] Most Amazing _____ To _____
[#] Facts About _____
[#] Essential Things For _____
[#] Key Benefits Of _____
[#] Examples Of _____ To Inspire You
[#] _____ That Will Motivate You Today
[#] _____ Ideas
[#] Reasons You Didn't Get _____

Pick of the Week/Month

- Editor's Pick Of The Week
- Readers Pick of The Month
- Fan Picks

Intriguing

- What No One Tells You About
- Questions
- You're Doing It Wrong:
- Are The ___?
- Why Are ___?

- Who On The Earth ____
- [#] Things That Make You Look Dumb On ____
- You Won't Believe
- What an ____ Really Looks Like
- Amazing Secrets
- Wish I had Known
- [#] Myths About

Questions

- Why Do You Want to ____?
- Is Your ____ Design To ____?
- Should You Create ____ To ____?
- Why You Need To ____ For ____
- Why Should You ____
- Is ____ Affecting Your ____
- Quiz: ____
- Today's Big Q: ____
- What The Heck Is ____?
- Why I Don't ____
- Who Else ____?

Comparison

- ____ VS ____ : Which Do You Need?
- ____ VS ____ : Which Is Really Better?
- Why ____ beats ____

Miscellaneous

- Throwback Thursdays: _____
- Best Tip Ever: _____
- The Only Tip You Need: _____

Link Love's Law of Reciprocity

There is another important step in the content creation process, and that is to hyperlink the keywords to other valuable, relevant content that belongs to someone else. That means do not link back to your website, social sites, or other content. You will link to other authoritative sites that benefit the reader and act as a compliment to the website being linked towards due to its content.

These are called backlinks. They are important because one of the major factors that can have an effect on search engine rankings is the backlinks pointing towards a website. You will want to people to link to your website and its pages and one of the best ways to do that is by including backlinks to other authoritative sites.

Giving link love through hyperlinking without the need for anything to be given back passes value to the other website and that puts the Law of Reciprocity in play. If you give link love, you will get link love in return. Some people are not clear about why you would give link love to others but not yourself. If you just link love yourself, you have a loving community of one. How far is that going to go? If you link love other authoritative sites, you build trust among your readers and if the site gives you link love in return, you increase your exposures to a broader community.

That was the Lisa Ann Landry simplification twists on backlinks and link love. Here is an excellent simplified technical explanation from Backlinko from their document *Google Ranking Factors Checklist.*

"Including your target keyword in strategic places on your page – like in your URL, in the beginning of your article and in H2 tags – sends a message to Google that your page is about that keyword.

ACTION STEP: Include your target keyword in the beginning of your title tag, in the first 100 words of an article and in an H2 or H3 tag.

The authority of your page – determined by the quality and quantity of inbound links – is by far the most important ranking signal that Google uses.

The fact is, unless your page is authoritative, Google isn't going to rank it (why would they?).

ACTION STEP: Incorporate white hat link building strategies like Guestographics to build your page's authority

As we already went over, a link's authority (as measured by the PR {Page Rank} of the linking page) is really important.

But Google is paying more and more attention to the relevancy of the links pointing to your site. In fact, an ex-

Google employee recently stated that "relevancy is the new PR").

So make sure that most of your links come from sites that are on the same topic as yours. So if you ran a site that sold organic food, make sure you're getting links from other pet-related sites...not sites about trucks and tattoos.

ACTION STEP: Focus on building links from authoritative AND relevant sites.

Grab your keywords, hashtags, titles, headings, and sub-headings and let's create some education-based marketing content in the next chapter.

Summary

In this chapter, you learned strategies on how to entice someone to consider reading your content by keyword optimizing your titles and headings. People on the Internet are not just busy, but they also have *extremely* short attention spans. When they go on the Internet searching among millions of choices, they must narrow down these options. So they focus on finding clues that they hope are sprinkled in the titles, headings and subheadings of the content found.

There is a method for crafting your titles that will help the content rank. The method requires including keywords at the beginning of the title. Since Google shows the first 60 to 70 characters of your title in the search results, it's ideal to have your keywords at the beginning of your titles. That way people looking at your content will scan search result pages and see the early words first.

The most evocative titles elicit an emotional response. Now you have a template for crafting all kinds of titles such as threats, instructions, teasers, lists, engagement, secrets and more. Equally as important to the titles are backlinks and the techniques associated with practicing link love. Remember, link love simply means linking to other authoritative sites that benefit the reader and act as a compliment to the website being linked towards due to its content. This practice is a major factor that can have an effect on your search engine rankings.

*"Provide good content and you'll earn
the right to promote your product."*
Guy Kawasaki

CHAPTER 9

A Remarkable KISS - Keep It Simple Success Model to Social Writing

I t's been said, "People in pain are looking for a painkiller!" I say show your prospects you are the pain reliever. Use the body of your content to address your reader's pain points. Here are a few questions to help you determine what can possibly trigger pain from your reader's perspective.

- What are they suffering from?
- What keeps them up at night?
- What are their fears?

- What are their frustrations, barriers, and complaints?

Your target market will spend money to minimize pain or to maximize pleasure. Yes, you can definitely deliver content that satisfies the pleasure points; however some would make the argument that Jon Burgstone and Bill Murphy, Jr. made in their article Why Customer Pain is Your Most Important Resource:

> *All things being equal, the more acute the pain or problem, the more likely it is that you'll be able to offer a compelling solution. The more compelling the solution, the more quickly the customer will pay. From an entrepreneur's perspective this means that it's often better to be in a "pain business" than a "pleasure business." There is simply more staying power in pain-solving businesses.*

As I write this a picture of Hugh Hefner and his harem of playboy bunnies flashed through my head. Hugh Hefner profited from the pleasure business. He has created a thriving empire from maximizing his audience's pleasure. The example certainly contradicts the notion there is simply more staying power in the pain-solving businesses.

Pain and pleasure points are not just part of the human equation; they are part of the business equation, too. For the entrepreneur, the pain point is to reduce cost, and the pleasure point is to increase business. Be on the lookout for new pains. Consider innovation. Even though it may be a solution to something else, innovation often creates a new pain point.

Let's work through the concept of pain points with the following illustration which highlights innovation and the resulting pain created. Consider the creation of cloud storage like Dropbox, Google Drive, and Microsoft One Drive; now, ask yourself: What pain points lead to the development of cloud storage? Look for the pain that would lead someone to use any of those products. Any ideas? Okay. We'll use mine.

How many computers do you have? I have my Sony VAIO, which I take with me on all my speaking engagements. I have my Dell 15Z that is usually in my office but is also the backup computer in case my traveling computer crashes. I also have a Sony PC Tablet that I carry with me all the time as a backup in case the Sony dies. Then I have my iPhone *(the latest one, I might add!)* which is pretty much a handheld tablet. Frequently, I work on which ever one is nearby. So if I'm upstairs in the office, that's the Dell. When I'm downstairs, it's the Sony VAIO. If I'm commuting on the bus or train, it's my iPhone or my Sony Tablet. I can work on my presentations and other files on anyone of these devices. When I started running into problems keeping my files synced *(pain point)* and even more horrifying when my laptop died, and I thought I lost all my files *(heart attack like pain point)* is what led me to start storing my files on the cloud drive.

With my files stored in the cloud, I have access to the most up-to-date files *(pleasure point)* not just from any of my devices *(pleasure point)* but any device that has computer access *(pleasure point)*.

Another pain point occurred when I developed a webinar for a client and needed the presentation edited and proofed. I could not e-mail her the file for editing and proofing because it was too big *(pain point)*, but I could share *(pleasure point)* the files through Dropbox. Dropbox is free, but you get limited free storage space. I really didn't want to pay to increase storage space *(pain point)*, and that caused me to look for another cloud storage solution.

I'm a huge Microsoft 360 fan. I've been using it for three years and just realized after using it for a year and a half or so that all users get 1 Terrabyte *(big honking pleasure point)* of cloud storage space as part of the subscription's service. That gives me enough space to store all my files and never run out of space. Can you see there is a pain point in all of this?

Personally, I was totally against storing my files in the cloud. I've heard the horror stories of cloud service providers going out of business *(pain point)* and customers losing all their data *(big honking pain point)*. What if the Dropbox goes out of business? What happens when you stop paying for the Microsoft 360? What happens when you don't have

Internet access? All of these issues are pain points. I always have a portable backup drive just in case *(pleasure point)*.

When identifying possible pain points think of things that people find disturbing, frustrating, urgent or uncomfortable. Then, with the pain clearly recognized, and in mind, develop pain relievers. Focus on healing. Let that be your guide as you craft content marketing that will relieve the pain. You're almost guaranteed to find something. Remember, customer pain is the ultimate renewable resource.

You may like to have a list of questions to uncover pain points. Although these listed will get you started, all you really need to do is reflect back to when you were in pain yourself and were searching for a pain reliever. Think of the questions you had in that situation. Did they look like some of these?

- Which doubts and hesitations did you have before completing the purchase?
- What kinds of things almost stopped you from making the purchase?
- What was your biggest challenge, frustration or problem when searching for the pain reliever to that particular problem?
- Which questions went unanswered because you couldn't find answers on the Internet?

When crafting content strive to deliver content that:

- **Satisfies a need**

  In the case of a health clinic's audience suppose their readers were told that if they don't change their ways, they will have to be on medication to control cholesterol, high blood pressure, or diabetes, etc. So what do they need? They need to know how to make changes and what changes to make.

- **Delivers a service**

  Suppose the health clinic delivers a variety of services and through content marketing not only do they educate their audience about health, they also indirectly educate people about the clinic's services.

- **Reduces stress**

  Imagine that you're really frustrated over healthcare options and don't know in what direction to go. By subscribing to the health clinic's content, you (the reader) have reduced the stress surrounding this issue because of all the tips, helpful websites and information provided by the clinic's content marketing.

- **Satisfies emotionally**

  The clinic's content marketing includes human interest stories of people in medical crisis and their stories of loss and survival. These stories touch people's heart and inspire hope.

Remember the Baskin Robbins analogy I used earlier? I recommend you look at your blog (and other lengthy content) as the gallon of ice cream. Once you have committed so much time and effort creating your content, don't just publish it on your website, think of a variety of ways to re-purpose it for different platforms.

Little pink spoons are a method of re-purposing. Take those little pink spoons (LPS) full of goodness from your content and find ways to repurpose it on the other social sites you are using. Here is an example. In January 2015, I published this piece of content (or should I say a gallon of ice cream) on LinkedIn.

The S.M.A.R.T. Rules for Using Social Media

Do you remember your first day of kindergarten? I can hardly remember my first day of kindergarten, those of you with children it might be easier to recall when you sent them to their first day of school. Just like your parents, you sent your kids off to school with all kinds of rules – "Come right home, I'm picking you up so stay at the front of the building, do what your teacher says!" You get my drift. As a social media strategist I've learned "SMART" rules apply to social media marketing just as they did when sending your kids off to school for the first time.

Many of my connections are quite social media savvy. This post is for small business owners, entrepreneurs, speakers, & consultants who are new to using social media. I want you to be aware that just as there were rules to abide by on the first day of Kindergarten there are rules for social media marketing.

Here are Lisa Ann's "SMART" Rules for Using Social Media:

S

Strategize *about the goals you want to accomplish by using social platforms. Do this before you start setting up your sights or start posting random, irrelevant content. Ultimately you will want to* <u>*Create a Social- Media Marketing Plan*</u>*.*

M

Manage *your time and use tools to assist you in creating and scheduling content. Many people will say that social media marketing is a waste of time. When you hear that make sure to ask why. My eyes always roll to the back of my head when these people say they've never used it. Many will agree with me that social media can be a time vampire and has* <u>*addictive properties*</u>*. That said, I can't tell you how important it is to set boundaries on how you spend your time.*

A

Add value to your social communities through your interactions and by posting valuable relevant content. If your currently using social media to stay connected with you family you've probably seen content that made you think – REALLY? Why would anybody post that? How is that information helpful or useful? Imaging the reaction your customer would have if you post such content. When your content adds value you accrue <u>social capital</u>.

R

Remember 'The law of Reciprocity' is very important to your Social Media success. As you accrue social capital The Law of Reciprocity is activated. Consequently you want to use <u>Reciprocity to Influence People, Drive Traffic and Make Sales</u>.

T

Treat the social space as a stage where you are visible GLOBALLY - 24/7.
Stay tuned as the "SMART social media rules continues with an elaboration on each of these SMART strategies. What are some of your SMART rules and guidelines for using social media?

Here is a sample of how I repurposed the content for other social sites such as Google+, Twitter, LinkedIn, and Facebook. One well-written piece of content can go a long way!

Used on Google +

Strategizing around the goals you want to accomplish on your social sites is a critical step in a social media marketing. It's especially important that you figure this out before you begin establishing your sites. Established strategy and goals will prevent you from posting random, irrelevant content. Learn more of <u>The S.M.A.R.T. Rules for Using Social Media</u> from your #socialmediastrategist.

Used on Twitter

1. As a social media strategist I've learned "SMART" rules apply to social media marketing what are some of your rules?
    #socialmediastrategist

2. There were rules for the 1st day of Kindergarten & there are rules for social media marketing http://ow.ly/JTJZG #socialmediastrategist

3. Manage time using tools to assist in creating & scheduling content my Fav Hootsuite http://ow.ly/JTLFN #socialmediastrategist

4. Do you feel social media is a time vampire & is addictive? http://ow.ly/JTMf7 #socialmediastrategist

5. Need to create a Social Media Marketing Plan hire me or do it free-1st answer these http://ow.ly/JTNlN #socialmediastrategist

Used on LinkedIn

When your content adds value, you accrue social capital #socialmediastrategist http://socialentrepreneurforum.com/index.php/tag/examples-of-social-capital

Used on Facebook

How would you answer these questions https://www.youtube.com/watch?v=tIrS2zkWXY4 #socialmediastrategist

How are you using Reciprocity to Influence People, Drive Traffic and Make Sales? #socialmediastrategist http://www.entrepreneurs-journey.com/11221/reciprocity/

Even though hashtags are no longer used on LinkedIn, I should have included ones like #socialmediastrategist or #socialmediastrategist. There are two reasons why. The first reason is when people see hashtags they know to search for them in other places, even if they aren't searchable from the current location. The second reason is that content published on the LinkedIn publishing platform indexes to Google search, which makes for great visibility for both the content and the hashtags. Don't forget to include your hashtags. The last step is to end with a call to action. I used what I call a social engagement call to action, which was the question: "What are some of your SMART rules and guidelines for using social media?" There is also a marketing call to action. Generating leads, qualified opportunities, and revenue dollars is the ultimate goal of content marketing. A marketing call to action is used to get people into your pipeline to take actions that will move them through your sales cycle.

Influencing Your Target Market to Do Something

Wikipedia defines *a call to action* (CTA) as "An instruction to the audience to provoke an immediate response, usually using an imperative verb such as "call now," "find out more" or "visit a store today." Calls to action are also used on social sites. Some argue that every form of communication with your customer should begin and/or end with a call to action.

I'm including a list of action words and action phrases to help you create the perfect call to action in your content.

Call to Action Words
- Add
- Buy
- Call
- Click
- Connect
- Join
- Learn
- Reply
- Share
- Start

Call to Action Phrases
- Get your free consultation

- I can't wait to hear from you
- Join now
- Learn more about us at . . .
- Start now
- Talk to an expert
- We'd like to hear from you

Summary

Most of us are naturally pain-averse and when in pain, we are highly likely to be looking for a pain reliever. Entrepreneurs who understand their customers' pain points find ways to address the pain through their products and services. Locating and understanding customers' pain points was traditionally performed during in person sales meetings; however, with today's online options, these pain points can be addressed through online content marketing. My hope is this chapter helped you to identify some ways to find customer pain points as well as methods to enhance your content so that you are seen as the pain reliever.

CHAPTER 10

Publish Content with Appropriate Frequency and Length

Social media marketing gurus say if you do nothing else with social media, you *have to* blog. I've consistently said that blogging is important because:

- It's a non-salesy method to do content marketing.
- Your blog is available on your website 24/7.
- It opens doors you can't open yourself.
- It creates presence and visibility for your brand online.

The last point deserves further explanation. I believe this is true because when working with my clients I've learned they don't really grasp this concept. Every time you publish blog content you create a unique time stamped and dated URL or Uniform Resource Identifier. Basically, it's the address on the web where your content lives. Imagine all the different characters who love the Uniform Resource Identifiers. Everyone on the Internet loves them, especially search engines. Search engines want to index them so that when we look for things on the Internet, we will get the most relevant results.

I'd like to share an example. As mentioned in the previous chapter, I wrote a post called *The S.M.A.R.T. Rules for Using Social Media.* Go ahead and conduct search for it on Google. (I'll wait). Did you notice the results return this URL? **https://www.linkedin.com/pulse/smart-rules-using-social-media-lisa-ann-landry?trk=prof-post.** An important point to keep in mind is that URLs help you to get found in search results and every time you publish blog content you create a unique time stamped and dated URL. URLs are also created when posting content on many of the social sites, another fact that many of my clients were unaware of. All that is to say, although you may not feel you're getting lots of leverage from your content marketing activity, think of it as planting seeds and dripping on the seeds you've planted. It takes time for the seeds to take root.

If you have the time and energy, creating blog content for each one of your editorial calendar entries is ideal. Unfortunately, it's unrealistic for many of you because of the time constraints you are already dealing with aside from your social media marketing activities.

At a minimum, create three blog posts a month. Include in the posts relevant pictures and videos (blog posts containing large visuals consistently show up as top performers). When it comes to visuals, remember, pictures and video are not the only options. Other options include a large custom image, infographic, or an embedded SlideShare presentation. Content best practices dictate your content is:

- Written at a 7th grade level with a reading ease of 60 or higher (Microsoft has a readability checker built into it, and you can also find readability checkers online).
- At a minimum 975 words to 2500 words (the optimal length for search engine optimization purpose).
- Developed with keyword optimized headings.
- Keyword optimized with three keywords or phrases per 300 words.
- Leveraging other valuable, relevant content by hyperlinking to other content or sites (not yours)

Edit Content to Repurpose for Different Platforms

Once you've created and published your gallon of ice cream (blog post), your next step will be to repurpose the content for the other social platforms where you're active. You will take little pink spoons of juicy goodness and post them to other sites. You will need to understand the content that's suitable for those sites. Here are a few examples for a few of the major social sites.

YouTube

YouTube is the world largest base of videos. Google has shifted its algorithms to favor videos, often putting YouTube videos near the top of its results. Much like your blog content generates visibility for your brand in search results, so do your videos. Each posted video creates a unique time stamped and dated URL. Every user can add their own video and can upload videos that are up to 15 minutes long. If you go through the process of verifying your YouTube account, Google gives you the possibility to upload videos up to 128GB of size and up to 11 hours long. I often tell people *just because you can, doesn't mean you should.*

Here are a few things to remember about videos. First, the social community has an attention span of seven seconds—that's shorter than the attention span of a gold fish!

Consequently, instead of creating long video content, consider creating a series of videos 3.5 to 5 minutes long with a call to action at the end of each video. Additionally, YouTube is loud and noisy very much like Times Square on New Year's Eve. While you want to stand out from the crowd and get their attention, you primarily want to focus on crafting content for your buyer persona and standing out to them based on your content. Again, I suggest a posting frequency of three videos a month.

Google Plus

Google Plus is a multifaceted social media network with a myriad of capabilities, from assisting with search engine rankings, to a constant flow of informative communication posted by Google Plus users in a continuous stream, 24 hours a day, and seven days a week. There are Chats, Circles, Hangouts, Games, Posts, Streams, Photos and so much more. As I said in a previous chapter, Google Plus is like the Mall of America—all the shops, cafes, big brand stores, specialty stores, etc. can be found in the specific Google Plus circles.

While text content length on Google Plus allows for 100,000 characters, the most popular types of content appears to be animated GIFs, photos, and videos all of which tends to include some text and URLs. Consider a frequency of two or three times per day.

Google is a great place to create communities (circles) of people with common interests. Remember as mentioned earlier, Google appears to give rank preference to its properties. Posting content on Google Plus will certainly index to its search engine, which will help you get found.

Twitter

Twitter is an information network made up of 140-character messages called tweets. It's like a Chamber cocktail party or a trade show where you can discover the latest news related to subjects you care about. It's also a microblog and similar to blogging, Google+ and YouTube, Twitter can impact search engine rankings.

Twitter allows 140 character status updates, but you should only use 100 to 120 characters to leave room for your community to *easily* share your tweets with their community. These are called RTs or retweets. Before I tell you how many tweets to do a day, I just want you to know that the Twitter newsfeed is like a fast-moving river of content. Most people are not sitting at the river watching what's passing by. When people really want to consume your content, they will put you in a list (like a customized group) and go look at the list to see the content from there. Also, remember if your tweets are valuable, relevant and useful, your followers will look forward to seeing your content.

Now, the big question is how frequently to post. I recommend a frequency of 10 to 20 tweets per day spread throughout the day (for presence and visibility). Visit the

Twitter newsfeed and you will see the most popular content is photos, videos, and text with URLs that send you to more meaty content.

Facebook

Facebook is one of the most popular of all social sites with over 1.5 billion active users. It's like a big family reunion picnic. Facebook allows status updates to be 63,206 characters. However, the optimum length for engagement is a post that contains 80 to 160 characters. *For your information: text posts get the least amount of engagement.* The most popular content is videos, photos, inspirational quotes, and memes. The content also includes URLs. Facebook is increasingly forcing brands to pay to play. Meaning if you want your content to show up in your fan's newsfeed you will have to purchase paid advertisements. However, if you have built a tribe of raving fans who are engaged, they will see your content and interact with it. The trick is that you need to be present so your post frequency should be one to three posts per day.

LinkedIn

LinkedIn is the professional networking site with a culture like that of the corporate boardroom. LinkedIn gives rank to profiles that are 100 percent complete, that are keyword optimized and that are active. Posting regular status updates, participating in groups, and/or publishing content will make you active and help you get found.

LinkedIn status updates allow for 700 characters, and the publishing platform functions like a blog. LinkedIn's publishing platform allows members, in addition to Influencers, to publish long-form posts about their expertise and interests. This allows you to further establish your professional identity by expressing your opinions and sharing your experiences. Given the fact you probably want to drive traffic to your website where your blog is hosted consider writing your content on the LinkedIn publishing platform much like you write for your blog but only write 975 characters. Think of it as an enticing pint that pairs well with your blog content. You want to tease your reader and leave them wanting more. For those who want more include links that drive them back to the gallon.

Frequency of posts on LinkedIn for status updates should be one a day seven days a week. Some recommend five days a week, but I find that seven days are appropriate when you are trying to reach small-business owners and entrepreneurs. Your blog posting frequency on LinkedIn should be between one to three times per month.

Other sites

There are others sites you may want to explore based on your target market, your product and services. These sites might include:

- **SlideShare** - www.slideshare.net

SlideShare began with a simple goal: To share knowledge online. Since then, SlideShare has grown to become the world's largest community for sharing presentations and other professional content. SlideShare was founded in October 2006 and acquired by LinkedIn in May 2012. It allows users to easily upload and share presentations, infographics, documents, videos, PDFs, and webinars. In the fourth quarter of 2013, the site averaged 60 million unique visitors a month and 215 million page views. SlideShare is among the top 120 most-visited websites in the world.

- **Pinterest** - https://about.pinterest.com

Pinterest is a free website that requires registration to use. Users can upload, save, sort, and manage images—known as pins—and other media content (e.g., videos and images) through collections known as pinboards. Pinterest acts as a personalized media platform. Users can browse the content of others on the main page.

- **Instagram** – https://instagram.com/

Instagram is an online mobile photo-sharing, video-sharing and social networking service that enables its users to take pictures and videos, and share them on a variety of social networking platforms, such as Facebook, Twitter, Tumblr and Flickr.

- **Podcasts**

The word *Podcast* comes from the combination of broadcast and iPod. The most popular format of a podcast is MP3.

> *"Podcasting is a form of audio broadcasting on the Internet. The reason it became linked with the iPod in the name was because people download the broadcasts (audio shows) to listen to on their iPods. However, you don't have to listen to podcasts only on iPods; you can use your computer with some music software such as Windows built-in Media Player or iTunes for Mac (which has a podcast library), or your smartphone, or even in your car. It really doesn't matter, as long as you have some way to play music on your computer you will be able to listen to podcasts."*

- **Webinar**

A Web-based seminar, it is a presentation, lecture, workshop or seminar transmitted over the Web using video conferencing software. A key feature of a Webinar is its interactive elements—the ability to give, receive and discuss information. Contrast with Webcast, in which the data transmission is one way and does not allow interaction between the presenter and the audience.

Summary

Your number one priority in content marketing is creating big gallons of ice cream. By now, you know that's blog content. Once that's complete, you repurpose your content by crafting little pink spoons of juicy goodness so that it's enticing yet suitable for the other social sites you use. Each social site has a culture and a language; the content you post needs to match the culture and you must post frequently enough for your fans to see and engage with your content. Content Marketing isn't just about crafting and posting content. You really want to interact and engage with your audience and vice versa. So read their content, reply to it, question it and share it. Being active on the social sites is not just about achieving visibility, it's about helping people to get to know like and trust you. When they do, they will buy from you.

"*My goal is to spark something within the reader and allow
it to initiate an idea they then can grow.*"
Warren Whitlock

CHAPTER 11

No! E-mail Marketing is Not Dead! It's Part of the Content Marketing

Toni Harris is a Marketing Strategist, a certified e-mail marketing trainer with *Constant Contact* and their number one Authorized Local Expert in North America. If you've ever heard talk about "The Turn Around Queen" that was Toni Harris. Toni agreed to an interview with me on e-mail marketing and this chapter is dedicated to e-mail marketing based upon our discussion. Toni will say although Constant Contact is a premier e-mail marketing product, this chapter addresses e-mail marketing in general. It includes guidelines you will want to follow if you intend to use e-mail to market your business.

> *"Social media and e-mail marketing go together like ice cream and cake."* Toni Harris

E-mail marketing is one of the most effective marketing tools. If you've ever met Toni you've experienced what a great face-to-face networker she is. Many people I've met who were great at this type of networking claimed to hate e-mail and social media as networking tools. Not Toni Harris, she contends, "Next to face-to-face networking, e-mail marketing is the second best form of networking. It is one of the most effective marketing tools around for small businesses. That's because everybody has e-mail. Although social media is hugely popular everybody doesn't have social media."

I did a little research to find out if her argument is really true and here is what I found out. "E-mail is the communications tool of choice in our hyper-connected age. Over 3.5 billion people around the world have an e-mail account (compared to 1.5 billion Facebook users). So if you've got a message or product to share, e-mail is the best way to do it."

Toni and I both agreed everybody we know, especially if they are in business, check their e-mails all day long. Some studies suggest the average person checks e-mail 15 times a day. That's why e-mail marketing is effective. Look at these statistics, "92% of U.S. adults use e-mail to communicate with others and 183 billion e-mails are sent and received each day. With half of the population afraid of being without their smartphone — a fear often referred to as nomophobia — e-mail plays a big role in helping people stay and feel connected.

Toni tells her audience to give the reader the message but don't make them go look for it. She reasons, "In social media if you post something to Facebook that's profound and I'm not on Facebook the moment you post it, then I missed it and I'm not going to go look for it. If you give me a message that is profound and you put it in my inbox I see you. You know the phrase, 'I see you' Well, 'I see you' when you show up in my inbox. I may or may not see your posts on social media."

Remember that Facebook and other social media sites don't show your posts to everybody who is your friend. If you want 100% of people to see you, you must use e-mail. Even if they don't open your e-mails they will see that you are still around. They see that you are still in business. When they need your product or service they know where to go to get you. Another thing to remember is customers who come to businesses via e-mail tend to shop more and spend more.

Important Suggestion: You Need An E-Mail Marketing Service Provider Now!!

Are you wondering why have an e-mail marketing service provider? Can't I just send my e-mails and newsletters from Yahoo, Gmail, Outlook or whatever e-mails service I have? An e-mail marketing service provider has things in place to get your e-mails through various types of filters like spam filters. Constant Contact has a 95% deliverability rate compared to the standard rate of 79%. This is one criteria for choosing an e-mail service provider. Another criteria is a guarantee the e-mail marketing service provider ensures the small business owner complies with the CAN SPAM act. The CAN-SPAM act has about eight rules that e-mail marketers must follow. The CAN-SPAM Act, was signed into law by President George W. Bush on December 16, 2003. It was the United States first national standard for the sending of commercial e-mail. The Federal Trade Commission (FTC) is required to enforce the acts provisions. CAN-SPAM is an acronym for _C_ontrolling the _A_ssault of _N_on-_S_olicited _P_ornography _A_nd _M_arketing Act of 2003.

The CAN-SPAM Act is a law that sets the rules for commercial e-mail, establishes requirements for commercial messages, gives recipients the right to have you stop e-mailing them, and spells out tough penalties for violations.

The CAN-SPAM Act applies to more than bulk e-mail. It covers all commercial messages, defined as "any electronic mail message the primary purpose of which is the commercial advertisement or promotion of a commercial product or service." It includes e-mail that promotes content on commercial websites. The law makes no exception for business-to-business e-mail. That means all e-mail—for example, a message to former customers announcing a new product line—must comply with the law.

Another reason to use an e-mail service provider has to do with the rule of opting out or unsubscribing. This is one of the "3 basic types of compliance defined in the CAN-SPAM Act. The other is content and sending behavior compliance." Unsubscribe has to do with giving people a way to get off your list immediately when they click unsubscribe or opt out. People who use traditional e-mail for marketing can't provide that options.

The second type is content compliance. This involves accurate "From" lines, relevant subject lines, and a legitimate physical address of the publisher and/or advertise. If the e-mail is sent by a third party, a legitimate physical address of the entity, whose products or services are promoted through the e-mail should be visible. If there is adult content it requires labeling it as such.

The third type is sending behavior compliance.

- A message cannot be sent:
    - ❖ Through an open relay
    - ❖ Without an unsubscribe option
    - ❖ To a harvested e-mail address
- A message
    - ❖ Cannot contain a false header
    - ❖ Should contain at least one sentence.
    - ❖ Cannot be null.
- Unsubscribe option should be below the message.

If someone complains to the FTC about your business e-mail practices you can be fined up to $16,000.00 per e-mail. So make sure you follow the rules listed below:

- Don't use false or misleading header information.
- Don't use deceptive subject lines.
- Identify the message as an ad.
- Tell recipients where you're located.
- Tell recipients how to opt out of receiving future e-mail from you.
- Honor opt out requests promptly.
- Monitor what others are doing on your behalf.

Toni admits that another reasons to use an e-mail service provider is to make your e-mails look better visually. With an e-mail service provider you have the ability to brand your e-mail, make your e-mail colorful, include videos, your business logo, and include PDFs in your e-mail and/or newsletter. You can't do these things with traditional e-mail programs.

Another thing that separates traditional e-mail programs from an e-mail service provider is the reporting provided. A good service provider will offer a report that includes information on who opened your e-mails, when, the links they clicked on, if the e-mail was forwarded, and if the videos were watched. You should get a report informing you of these kinds of things for every e-mail that goes out.

Constant Contact allows your audience to share your message on their social sites. This is really powerful. Imagine you send me an e-mail newsletter and I really like what it says, all I have to do is click the Facebook link and I can share your newsletter on my own Facebook page. This exposes your business and content to a broader audience who might become a fan or client.

Toni points out you should have permission to e-mail people. "E-mail is effective because it's permission-based. The people on your e-mail list have given you the go-ahead to send them messages. They're bought in. And, with the prevalence of smartphones and tablets, they're always listening. In fact, e-mail is the number-one activity for people on their phones. The "new inbox" is always on. People check e-mail constantly, wherever they are, and that enables you to stay connected."

There are two types of permission explicit and implied. Explicit permission is when people opt in to your e-mail list, by signing up at your website, submitting their e-mail address, texting or scanning a QR code to join your e-mail list. There is also implied permission. This is given anytime a purchase is made online, a business card is dropped into a fishbowl or registration is completed on a sign in sheet. Sometime people get aggravated when they start getting e-mails due to giving implied permission. Toni says if someone adds you to their list in that way don't make a big deal of it. If you don't want to be on the list simply unsubscribe.

How to write rich e-mail subject lines that people actually open Using The Triple S Formula

Toni recommends the *Triple S Formula* for writing rich e-mail subject lines that compels people to actually open them. According to Toni the *Triple S Formula* is to make it *a Short, Sweet, Surprise!* Toni admits even she has trouble with short subject lines and confesses the best one she ever saw came from someone who coaches entrepreneurs. Her subject line was *"I'm going out of business."* Toni was so distraught over the news she rushed to open the e-mail. The body of the e-mail read, "I hate to hear business owners say this." That short, sweet, surprise of a subject line has an 80% open rate. She pulls me aside and whispers *"Subject lines that are a little sexy are not bad either."*

Some rules to follow for the subject lines include a title length of 30 characters or less. Also avoid using a lot of exclamation points. You don't want the e-mails to come off as spam because your message might get blocked. These common spam triggers are sure to block our message they are: !!!, $$$, 100% Free, and ALL CAPITALS. For a more complete listing of spam triggers check out the article written by Karen Rubin entitled *The Ultimate List of E-mail SPAM Trigger Words.* Here's the link:

http://blog.hubspot.com/blog/tabid/6307/bid/30684/The-Ultimate-List-of-E-mail-SPAM-Trigger-Words.aspx

How to Identify Yourself Using The E-mail "from" and "subject" line

Research indicates there are two things people look at to determine whether or not they should open your e-mail. Those two things are the *from* and the *subject* lines. Make sure your *from* line identifies you in a way people know you best. For example, I could put in my *from* line "The Turn Around Queen" but nobody would know who that is. So instead I use "Toni Harris the Turn Around Queen" to get my name and tagline out there. If your company name is the most recognized use that name. What I've started seeing lately, which I don't like, is people put a subject in the *from* line with my name and put a message there. For example: "lisaalandry, Compare amazing deals on SUVs."

As far as the subject lines, Constant Contact offers 12 ideas for super subject lines. It should be easy to remember because they use the mnemonic subject lines:

- Snappy – stay short and sweet
- Urgent – be timely
- Bold – use strong, impactful statements
- Joking – make your readers laugh
- Emotional –pull at their heartstrings

- Celebratory – announce something new and exciting
- Teasing – pique interest
- Loud – throw in some onomatopoeia
- Inquisitive – ask them a questions
- Negative – turn a negative into a positive
- Eccentric – don't blend in, stand out
- Sincere – always be genuine

How to make E-mails right for Mobile magic

About 70% of people are opening e-mails on their mobile devices. Consequently, it's important that e-mails are mobile ready. That means when someone clicks on items in that e-mail template they should be active links that whisk them off to other sites. That's what makes a template mobile ready. While your template should be mobile ready, it's not automatic. It's another one of those qualities of a good e-mail service provider. Your e-mail service provider should provide templates that are mobile ready.

How to avoid making more salesy, slimy, and sleazy e-mails

Toni recommends creating e-mails newsletters that educate the reader. Educational in terms of your business, industry, or even something personal—but don't sell. Her formula for a good newsletter is to keep it short. No one wants to read your book or dissertation. If you have ten tips for something, deliver a tip a month, or a tip a week. Don't deliver all ten tips in one e-mail newsletter because the majority of people are not inclined to read it. Your reader knows you're an expert, leverage that position to educate your reader not sell them. On the flipside for the people who are interested in contacting you or purchasing your product or service, don't forget to put your contact information and include a little sentence about what you do. This communicates to your reader that people can get in touch with you. For example: Need help? Contact me for social media marketing strategies to grow your business.

What length should the e-mails be?

Abraham Lincoln was able to communicate to a divided nation through the Gettysburg Address the importance of humanity and equality in 271 words. Yet some e-mails and newsletters I receive are so long it's like reading a freaking novel. Who has time for that? According to Constant Contact, "E-mails with about 20 lines of text and three or fewer images received the highest click-through rate."

Toni stands by what she has said all along *less is more.* Her recommendation for newsletter length is 300 words or less. She suggests that it is even better to provide a video tip 2 minutes or less within your newsletter. Toni illustrates that "All I want to do is a pageant wave in people's inbox." The wonderful thing about e-mails is that 100% of the people see e-mails from you, even if only 20% of the people open them. Because you see every e-mail that comes to you, a decision has to be made as to whether you're going to open it or not. The second you see Toni's name in the e-mail a picture of her flashes in your head whether you open me or not.

What is the deal with e-mail signatures?

The guideline to follow for an e-mail signature is *always have one!* Every e-mail should include contact information, your website, and social media links. A good quality professional photo will be part of your e-mail especially if the entrepreneur is in a speaking and consulting business like we are. Having a good quality professional photo is important.

Is there such a thing as a one-size-fits-all e-mail?

No, there is no such thing as a one-size fits all e-mail. This is a challenge for many. Because a good e-mail marketer, one who is doing it the right way, has a separate e-mail for different lists. A quality e-mail service provider gives their users the ability to have multiple lists so they can send separate e-mails to customers and prospects. So, again, one size does not fit all. The challenge is making separate e-mails for those different segments.

Establishing the delivery frequency of E-mail campaigns

The delivery frequency of your e-mail campaigns heavily depends on the type of business. 90% of businesses need only send a monthly newsletter and the occasional events announcement. For example, when you're having a networking event or something of that nature send an e-mail about it. Some business do lend themselves to weekly e-mails or a tip of the week. Such businesses often have a weekly sale, or a daily special with coupons and discounts. Otherwise, daily is too much, weekly is almost too much, unless you really have something to say. Toni advises monthly or bi-monthly at the most.

See E-mail marketing as an amazing sure-fire Lead Generator

E-mail marketing can be an amazing Lead Generator. You can make this happen by using marketing techniques. One such technique is to include the *forward to a friend* button in the e-mail newsletter. When it's forwarded to a friend that friend can join your list. Constant Contact has a feature called an autoresponder that automatically sends a welcome e-mail to new list members. The welcome e-mail can include a free gift like a relevant PDF document, for instance, *Toni's 52 Tips to Drastic Online Results for Your Business.*

The system is designed to allow you to entice people to join your list. Lead generation is created by giving them something free. What's really awesome is that it's automatic. That means you don't have (nor do you want) to *manually* send the gift out to everyone who joins your list. Make sure your e-mail service provider has some kind of autoresponder so that when people join your list you can give them a gift. By giving a gift people are more apt to join you list.

An autoresponder is a computer program that is set to send a series of e-mails that are automatically scheduled to go to the e-mail address after someone has joined the list. Once you've joined the list, the autoresponder is set to send a weekly e-mail tip to you like the 10 drastic steps for marketing success. For ten weeks someone can get an e-mail tip, it can be weekly or biweekly or as often as you want. What a fantastic time-savings method to setup the auto responder and put it on autopilot so that you don't have to do it manually. It's also great for scheduling your monthly newsletter.

In terms of lead generation, there are tools that measure how many leads were generated from e-mails. With reporting features, you can tell who forwarded your e-mails and who they forwarded it to. There are data in the reports that inform you who joined your list recently and where they came from. Without an e-mail service provider like Constant Contact, you would have to go back to look at your contacts to see who or if that person joined. Clearly, an e-mail service provider makes lead generation easier.

How to guarantee interactivity in your e-mails

One thing you can do to make e-mails more interactive is to put videos in them. Videos are key. Talking head videos are fine, too. The other way to encourage interactivity is to hyperlink things like keywords and pictures. People can click on them and be taken to a website, blog or something of that nature. Preferably the link should take them to your website. Links are a great thing to include in your newsletter because they can drive people to your website.

We all know you can build a website and create blogs, but that doesn't mean it's like *The Field of Dreams* and they are just going to magically come to your site. If you are blogging, using e-mail marketing is critical to drive traffic to your content. Just remember to give me your message in the e-mail newsletter. Don't make me go look for it. A technique that Toni likes to use is to take the first paragraph of blog content—by now you know I would call this a little pink spoon—and put it in the newsletter template that has a "click here to read more" button. Clicking the button drives the reader to your blog site.

How to easily integrate e-mail, newsletters and social media

E-mail marketing, newsletters, and social media all go together. According to Toni, E-mail marketing, and social media go together like ice cream and cake. She says, "I can have ice cream separately, and I can have cake separately but when I put them together mmm, good. E-mail marketing is about giving people the message. Social media marketing is about being present in a community, especially among people who aren't on your e-mail list."

In both situations, you have to show up but the trick is to drive people from your social sites to your e-mail. The key point to understand here is you can control your e-mail list. You don't have that same kind of control over your connections on social sites. Suppose you don't like what your e-mail service provider is doing or the features they have. In that case, you can take your list and go to another e-mail service provider. With social media, you're at the mercy of whatever these free sites decide. For instance, if *Facebook* goes out of business tomorrow I've lost those 5,000 friends.

While I can't say this is true of all e-mail service providers, I can say that with Constant Contact social media integration features are built in. Let's use the example of an e-newsletter. The moment a newsletter goes out in e-mail, I can also link it to LinkedIn, Facebook, and Twitter. One of the features I love about Constant Contact is that each e-mail newsletter creates a web page that can be shared making it incredibly easy to integrate e-mail, newsletters, and social media.

These are just a few tips on getting started with an e-mail marketing strategy. The goal here is to also help you see how e-mail marketing is part of your content marketing strategy and that having an integrated approach will not only save you time but generate traffic and clients.

Toni has been advocating for me to join her as an Authorized Local Expert. I decided to take her advice and now I am also an Authorized Local Expert with Constant Contact and would love to help you make it part of your content strategy. Become a client or at least giving it a test drive. Here is how:

http://www.constantcontact.com/index.jsp?pn=thesnccwa
y.

CHAPTER 12

Quick Simple Easy Social Checklists to Save Your Time and Energy

I wrote this chapter for those of you who are in a rush to get to it. Yes, I know you would love to read the whole book but you simply don't have time. If you just want the highlights so you can get started, this chapter was written just for you. It's a checklist of the key points from every chapter. Of course, you can find depth in the associated chapter.

Remember your content marketing depends on you and your willingness to follow the strategies I've outlined in this book.

Chapter 1:
A Spotlight on What Content
Marketing Actually Is

1. **What is content marketing?**

   ✓ The most commercially important digital marketing trend in the past few years.
   ✓ More cost-effective than ever before.
   ✓ Technology allows you to reach your audience. through blogs, social media, e-Newsletters, videos, infographics, mobile apps.
   ✓ Used to improve customer relationships, increase brand loyalty, boost engagement and raise brand awareness.
   ✓ Used to attract, acquire, and engage your target audience to generate profitable customer activity for your business.
   ✓ Creating and sharing free valuable content to attract and convert prospects into repeat buyers.

2. **Don't be salesy, pushy, slimy or sleazy**

   ✓ Being pushy, salesy, slimy, and sleazy using the social sites, ticks off your friends, fans, prospects, and followers.

✓ Many people simply disconnect from you.

✓ You may even be reported as a spammer.

✓ Losing those connections can be costly to your brand.

✓ Instead build a relationship with your readers that help them to know, like, and trust your brand.

3. Practice the Law of Reciprocity

✓ Remember, it is about giving or sharing your knowledge, wisdom, and expertise with others.

✓ Serve with an open heart and aid your community in whatever way you can, with the underlying belief the same energy you put out will somehow be returned to you.

✓ Start to identify those who operate with the Law of Reciprocity philosophy in mind.

✓ Engage the Law of Reciprocity to achieve credibility, influence and trust on the Internet with the intention of creating raving fans and customers who buy your products and services and tell others.

✓ Use the Baskin-Robbins method of education-based marketing.

4. Baskin Robbins Little Pink Spoons

✓ The little pink spoons are strategically placed throughout the store to entice you (Baskin-Robbins' target market) to sample their flavors.

✓ One of the easiest places to do education-based marketing (content marketing) is through blogging.

✓ Think of your blog as the gallon of ice cream in the Baskin-Robbins analogy.

✓ Leverage it by sprinkling LPS of juicy morsels of goodness from your blog around to the other social platforms you're using.

✓ Content Marketing covers hard to ignore benefits.

Chapter 2
See the Content Marketing Imperative You Need to Know

5. **The Content Marketing Imperative**

✓ This is about getting found by your prospect and clients.

✓ One of the best ways to generate presence in search results.

✓ Use the Baskin-Robbins Little Pink Spoon Method.

✓ Educate your target market and entice them with juicy morsels of valuable, relevant content.

✓ Start with your blog.

✓ When your target market finds your juicy content, they share it, and that's how it spreads.

6. Content spreads to create exposure

✓ Raving fans can cause your brand message to spread and impact thousands of people.

✓ Mainstream media may listen to those raving fans and may write about you in their newspaper and magazine articles, in TV and radio reports, and in blog posts.

✓ You can spread you message with a Webcast

✓ You can spread you message with an e-announcement to your opt in e-mail list.

✓ Make sure to include links that drive people to your website.

7. Content marketing builds trust

✓ It's a mistake to use the social sites to do push marketing.

✓ Don't be salesy, pushy, slimy, and sleazy on the social sites or you lose fans.

✓ Use inbound marketing techniques to build trust with you community.

    ✓ Inbound marketing techniques include website, webcasts, podcast, blogging, e-mail marketing, e-newsletters, etc.

8. **Content marketing informs buyers**

    ✓ In the purchase cycle, most of us do product research online first before we buy.

    ✓ Buyers look online at trusted sources to gather all the information to aid them in making an informed decision.

    ✓ Trusted sources include social sites where we are connected with friends and family to seek their opinions and other trusted sources for information gathering such as blogs, YouTube, etc.

    ✓ Content marketing is important in creating presence and trust.

    ✓ Presence helps us get found by the people who are willing to pay for what we have to offer.

Chapter 3
Getting Started Guide
to Content Marketing

9. **Content marketing is not like a useless piece of stone**

   ✓ You may have been told that content marketing is no good and it doesn't work.
   ✓ It works when you strategize, create a plan, and work the plan with committed consistent effort.

10. **How to create your content marketing masterpiece**

    ✓ Create a content marketing strategy.
    ✓ Identify keywords.
    ✓ Prime to use hashtags.
    ✓ Keyword optimize your titles and content.
    ✓ Publish valuable, relevant, quality content.

11. **Each platform has unique features, culture, language and tone**

    ✓ When blogging, write to speak to your target market providing them with valuable and relevant content that satisfies their pain points.
    ✓ The culture of YouTube is like Times Square on New Year's Eve. It's crowded, loud and noise. That means you will have to find a way

to stand out from the crowed to be seen by your target audience.

✓ Google Plus culture is like a huge super shopping mall and in it is every walk of life, culture, religious and social belief system. Google circles are the equivalent to stores in the mall.

✓ The culture of Twitter is like a chamber cocktail party or a trade show. It's a microblog that allows users to exchange small elements of content such as short sentences, individual images, or video links.

✓ The culture of Facebook is like a big family reunion picnic. It's totally appropriate on the Facebook business page to market and sell your products and services. You should do so by tapping into the picnic culture using contests, sweepstakes, games, videos, photos, polls and stories.

✓ LinkedIn is the premier business networking site think of the culture like that of a corporate boardroom.

12. Goals to accomplish on the social sites

✓ Blog: Your goal is to dominate search engines. Blogging is really the secret sauce to social media success and a big part of your content marketing success . . . that, and the little pink spoon.

✓ YouTube: Your goal is to be seen.

✓ Google Plus: The goal is to get found in the search engines.

✓ Twitter: Your goal is to share what's going on.

✓ Facebook: Your goal is to build a tribe of raving fans.

✓ LinkedIn: Your goal is to expand and leverage your professional network.

Chapter 4
Create a Content Marketing Strategy

13. Creating successful content strategy

✓ Requires producing content that corresponds with the concerns and interest of your buyer personas.

✓ A buyer persona is a semi-fictional representation of your ideal customer based on market research and real data about your existing customers.

✓ The content strategy focuses on creating buyer persona-driven content that helps prospects get to know, like, and trust you.

✓ Content needs to be compelling, and deliver real value because such content creates leads that convert to customers.

✓ The content's purpose is to deliver information that makes the prospect more intelligent or solves day-to-day challenges.

✓ The purpose of content strategy is to facilitate the consistent delivery of interesting stories. The end result is that you will attract and retain the attention of the targeted audience that you want to reach.

✓ Content strategy is planning for the creation, delivery, and governance of useful, usable content.

14. Picture your target market

✓ Helps you tailor your content to meet the needs of your buyer persona.

✓ Use buyer persona tool developed by marketing strategist Ardath Albee called Up Close & Persona™. Her website address:
http://www.upcloseandpersona.com.

15. Clues to target market pain points

✓ Your target market gives you clues to help you identify their pain points.

✓ You can gain clues from the types of questions they always ask about your product, industry or service.

✓ There are clues in subject matter they bring up and the content platforms they go to for answers.

✓ There are clues hiding in plain sight at your website under the FAQ Tab.

✓ You have content for your buyer personas you've already created. It's everywhere in your work environment as well as online in printed and digital formats.

16. The company content marketing Scavenger Hunt

✓ Have a company content scavenger hunt.

✓ A scavenger hunt is a game in which a list defining specific items, which the participants—individuals or teams—seek to gather all items on the list.

✓ The content is anything that has to do with your industry, company, its people, products, and services.

✓ Video record the scavenger hunt and do group presentations on what they found.

✓ See Scavenger Hunt List for items.

✓ There are years of content in the heads of your employees and customers; find ways to get it out. You can do so by doing interviews, surveys, and testimonials.

✓ Capture content in pictures and video format from company sales, promotions and charity events.

✓ Use a Mindmap to get additional content ideas out as well as organize the content you've gathered during the scavenger hunt.

Chapter 5
Steps to Identify Key Words

17. Steps to defining key words

✓ Keywords are single words, or more commonly strings of words, that represent the content of a web page and how people ask for web content.

✓ Keywords are strategically selected by optimizers and are intended to help your web content communicate in a way that resonates with humans and Google search spiders.

✓ You will incorporate the keywords both in the body of your text and in the headings and sub-headings in a subtle natural way.

✓ If you want to go to Google jail use keywords to trick and mislead readers and Google.

18. Who cares about keywords?

✓ People with problems.

✓ People who don't know you exist.

✓ By including keywords and phrases in your content, you are leaving breadcrumbs that lead people with problems to your product or service that can help them.

19. How to identify keywords

✓ Start thinking like your buyer personas, your customers, and people who have the problems you fix.

✓ Make a broad list of keyword and keyword phrases they would use when they search on the problems that your product or service would correct or resolve.

✓ Think like a potential customer who doesn't know your business exists.

✓ List targeted phrases too, for example "eye glasses or contact lenses—alternatives."

20. Are these really keywords?

- ✓ Just because you think your customers use certain keywords or phrases doesn't make it true.
- ✓ Use tools to research the keywords and phrases you intend to use in your content marketing
- ✓ Use tools like Google Keyword Planner, Topsy or other free keyword tools.
- ✓ Every time you create long-form content (this is your lengthier content such as blog posts) you will conduct keyword research.
- ✓ This research is critical to inform you of what keywords to include in content you create.

Chapter 6
Planning Hashtags

21. What are hashtags?

- ✓ A hashtag is a set of characters used to organize content in social media.
- ✓ It's a word or phrase prepended by (#) and is followed by some characters.
- ✓ The hashtag is so recognized that it was added to the Oxford dictionary in 2010.

✓ Using a hashtag makes the content searchable if that content contains that unique acronym or phrase.

✓ Think of hashtags as putting a label on a file folder and all the content in the file folder is related to the hashtag.

✓ When you see hashtags on social sites just click on them and you can see all the conversations.

22. Planning for hashtags?

✓ Hashtag rules dictate that you use no more than three hashtags in your content.

✓ Conduct hashtag research before deciding which hashtags to use in your content.

✓ Avoid lengthy hashtags because people won't use them. Your goal is to get your friends, fans and followers to use them, too. That means you have to make it easy.

✓ See the list of sources for hashtag research in the reference section of this book.

23. Hashtag marketing strategies?

✓ Be strategic when choosing hashtags and look for ways to connect your brand with various popular and incredibly visible topics.

✓ Use brand specific hashtags. These are hashtags that you make for your own business.

✓ Use campaign specific hashtags such as the name of your current marketing campaign.

✓ Use content specific hashtags in categories such as: Product, Lifestyle, Event, and Location.

✓ Once you identify your keywords, hashtags and topic themes, you can lay it out on an editorial calendar.

✓ An editorial calendar is used by bloggers, publishers, businesses, and groups to control publication of content across different media. Its primary purpose is to control the publication of content to ensure regular appearance of content that interests readers and advertisers.

Chapter 7
Using Editorial Calendars
for Planning Content

24. Editorial Calendars for planning content

✓ Good time management means participating on the right social platforms.

✓ The participation decisions are made based on your target market, platforms they use, Google pages rank, and SEO advantage.

✓ You will likely blog, and use the major social sites such as Facebook, Twitter, LinkedIn, YouTube, Google+, and Pinterest.

✓ Plan in advance what your content themes, keywords, and hashtags will be for all your social sites.

✓ Plan to lay them out on a 12-month Editorial Calendar

25. Why use an Editorial Calendar?

✓ An editorial calendar is a listing of your planned content including the themes and hashtag you intend to use in your content marketing.

✓ It's a system to prevent the drain on your time by suppling you with weeks and even months of content themes, keywords, and hashtags that you can leverage to create content that carries you through the year.

✓ The editorial calendar is a major time saver.

26. How to use an Editorial Calendar

✓ Go back to your Mindmap and select appropriate content themes for your brand.

✓ Select a theme of the day, theme of the week, or theme of the month for 12 months.

✓ Plot content themes, themes for promotions, sales and events, keywords, and hashtags on the 12 month editorial calendar.

✓ Craft or repurpose content (from scavenger hunt) for your blog and social sites using content that corresponds with your themes.

✓ From the blog, the goal is to get your fans to opt in to your list to receive your e-mail newsletter. Research shows that when you are able to capture prospect data and get them to opt in to your newsletter you'll experience a 50% increase in your sales.

✓ Use your e-mail newsletter to offer coupons, discounts, and extra special content that can't be found anywhere else.

Chapter 8
Keyword Optimize

27. Your titles and content

✓ Take keywords you researched and use them in content title, headings and subheadings.

✓ People skim your titles, headings and subheadings looking for clues trying to quickly decide if they should read further.

✓ Search engines put more weight on the early words in titles. You will want your keywords near the beginning of the title because you are more likely to rank well.

✓ People looking at your content will scan search result pages and see the early words first so put your keywords at the beginning of your titles

✓ Google shows the first 60 to 70 characters of your title in the search results.

✓ It's also important to include your keyword(s) within the first 100 words of your content.

28. Content Marketing T.I.T.L.E.S.

✓ Titles are important to capture your reader's attention.

✓ Good titles evoke an emotional response, ask a question, or promise something (that the content fulfills).

✓ Lead titles and content with keywords or keyword phrases.

✓ Types of Titles: Teasers, Instructions, Threats, Lists, Engagement, Secrets.

29. Content Marketing

✓ Tips

✓ How to

✓ List Titles

✓ Pick of the Week / Month.
✓ Intriguing
✓ Questions
✓ Comparison
✓ Miscellaneous

30. Link Love's Law of Reciprocity

✓ Hyperlink the keywords to other valuable, relevant content that belongs to someone else.
✓ Link to other authoritative sites that benefit the reader and act as a complement to the website being linked towards due to its content.
✓ These are called backlinks; the act is also referred to as giving link love (hyperlinking without the need for anything to be given back passes value to the other website).
✓ When you give link love to other authoritative sites, you build trust among your readers and the site that gives you link love in return increase your exposures to a broader community.

Chapter 9
Using the Keep It Simple
Success Model to Write

31. Matching Content Marketing to Pain Points

- ✓ People in pain are looking for a painkiller.
- ✓ Use the body of your content to address your reader's pain points.
- ✓ Reader's pain triggers:
  - o What are they suffering from?
  - o What keeps them up at night?
  - o What are their fears?
  - o What are their frustrations, barriers, and complaints?
- ✓ Deliver content that:
  - o Satisfies a need.
  - o Delivers a service.
  - o Reduces stress.
  - o Emotionally satisfies.
- ✓ Once you have committed so much time and effort creating content don't just publish the content on your website, think of a variety of ways to repurpose it for different platforms.

32. Target Market to Do Something

- ✓ In marketing, a call to action (CTA) is an instruction to the audience to provoke an immediate response.
- ✓ Calls to action are also used on social sites

✓ Every form of communication with your customer should begin and/or end with a call to action.

✓ There are Call To Action Words
- o Call
- o Reply
- o Click
- o Learn
- o Connect
- o Add
- o Join
- o Buy
- o Start
- o Share

✓ There are Call to Action Phrases
- o Get your free consultation
- o I can't wait to hear from you
- o Join now
- o We'd like to hear from you
- o Start now
- o Learn more about us at . . .
- o Talk to an expert

Chapter 10
Publish Content with Appropriate Frequency and Length

33. Your Number One Priority

- ✓ If you do nothing else with social media at least blog.
- ✓ It's a non- salesy method to do content marketing.
- ✓ Your blog is available on your website 24/7.
- ✓ It opens doors you can't open yourself.
- ✓ It creates presence and visibility for your brand online.

34. Blogging Frequency and Length

- ✓ At a minimum, create one blog posts each month; however, three would be better.
- ✓ Include in the posts relevant pictures and videos, large custom images, infographics, or an embedded SlideShare presentation, etc.
- ✓ Write at a 7th grade level with a reading ease of 60 or higher.
- ✓ Write a minimum 975 words to 2500 words.
- ✓ Develop keyword optimized headings.
- ✓ Keyword optimize by using three keywords or phrases per 300 words.

✓ Leverage other valuable, relevant content by hyperlinking to other authoritative content or sites.

35. Edit content to repurpose for different platforms

✓ Repurpose the content for the other social platforms you are active on by taking little pink spoons of juicy goodness and post them to other sites.

✓ YouTube: Each video you post creates a unique time stamped and dated URL. Publish a series of videos 3.5 to 5 minute videos with a call to action at the end of each video 1 to 3 times a month.

✓ Google Plus: While text content length on Google+ allows for 100,000 characters, the most popular types of content appears to be animated GIFs, photos, and videos all of which tends to include some text and URLs. Consider a frequency of two or three times per day Google appears to give rank preference to its properties.

✓ Twitter: Twitter allows 140 character status updates, optimal length for retweets 100 to 120 characters. Use a tweet frequency of 10 to 20 tweets per day spread throughout the day (for presence and visibility).

✓ Facebook: Facebook allows status updates to be 63,206 characters. The optimum length for engagement is a post that contains 80 to 160 characters. Text posts get the least amount of engagement. The most popular content is photos, videos, inspirational quotes, and memes. The content also includes URLs. Post one to three times per day.

✓ LinkedIn: LinkedIn gives high rank to profiles that are 100 percent complete, that are keyword optimized and that are active. Posting regular status updates, participating in groups, and or publishing content will make you active and help you get found. LinkedIn status updates allow for 700 characters, and the publishing platform functions like a blog at minimum write 975 words. Frequency of posts on LinkedIn should be one a day, seven days a week. It can be status updates, participation in groups or posting blog content.

✓ Other sites to consider:
   o SlideShare
   o Pinterest
   o Instagram
   o Podcasts
   o Webninars

Chapter 11
No! E-mail marketing is not dead!

36. E-mail marketing is not dead! It's part of the content marketing strategy

- ✓ E-mail marketing is one of the most effective marketing tools for small businesses because everybody has e-mail.
- ✓ Over 3.5 billion people around the world have an e-mail account (compared to 1.5 billion Facebook users).
- ✓ The average person checks e-mail 15 times a day; that's why e-mail marketing is effective.
- ✓ 92% of U.S. adults use e-mail to communicate with others and 183 billion e-mails are sent and received each day.
- ✓ Give the reader the message but don't make them go look for it. They will see it when you show up in their inbox. They may or may not see your posts on social media.
- ✓ If you want 100% of people to see you, you must use e-mail.

37. You need an E-mail Marketing Service Provider now!

- ✓ A service provider has things in place to get your e-mails through various types of filters like spam filters.
- ✓ Constant Contact has a 95% deliverability rate compared to the standard rate of 79%.
- ✓ E-mail service providers ensure the small business owner complies with the CAN SPAM Act.
- ✓ The CAN-SPAM Act has rules that e-mail marketers must follow and fines for violations up to $16,000.00 per e-mail.
  - o Don't use false or misleading header information.
  - o Don't use deceptive subject lines.
  - o Identify the message as an ad.
  - o Tell recipients where you're located.
  - o Tell recipients how to opt out of receiving future e-mail from you.
  - o Honor opt out requests promptly.
  - o Monitor what others are doing on your behalf.
- ✓ An e-mail service provider makes your e-mails more visually appealing.
- ✓ An e-mail service provider delivers reports that include information on who opened your e-mails, when, the links they clicked, if the e-mail

was forwarded, and if the videos were watched, etc.

✓ Includes social sharing features.

✓ E-mail is effective because it's permission-based and the number-one activity for people on their mobile phones.

38. How to write rich e-mail subject lines that people actually open

✓ Use the Triple S formula for writing rich e-mail subject lines.

✓ Make it - a Short, Sweet, Surprise.

✓ Make the subject lines title length of 30 characters or less.

✓ Avoid the common spam triggers:!!!, $$$, 100% Free, and ALL CAPTITALS.

✓ Read The Ultimate List of E-mail SPAM Trigger Words" by Karen Rubin.

39. How to use the e-mail *from* and *subject* lines to effectively identify yourself

✓ Research show that there are two things that people look at to determine whether or not they should open your e-mail, the "from" and the "subject" lines.

✓ Make sure your *from* line identifies you in a way people know you best.

✓ 12 ideas for super subject lines:
- o Snappy – stay short and sweet
- o Urgent – be timely
- o Bold – use strong, impactful statements
- o Joking – make your readers laugh
- o Emotional –pull at their heartstrings
- o Celebratory – announce something new and exciting
- o Teasing – pique interest
- o Loud – throw in some onomatopoeia
- o Inquisitive – ask them a questions
- o Negative – turn a negative into a positive
- o Eccentric – don't blend in, stand out
- o Sincere – always be genuine

✓ About 70% of people are opening e-mails on their mobile devices, so make sure your e-mails are mobile ready.

40. How to avoid making salesy, slimy, and sleazy e-mails

✓ Creating e-mail newsletters that educate the reader in terms of your business, industry, or even something personal. Remember, don't sell and keep it short.

✓ What length should the e-mails be? E-mails with about 20 lines of text and three or fewer images received the highest click-through rate. 300 words or less including a video tip 2 minutes or less.

✓ What is the deal with e-mail signatures? The guideline to follow for an e-mail signature is to have one in every e-mail. It should include contact information, your website, social media links, and a good quality professional photo.

✓ Is there such thing as a one-size-fits-all e-mail? A good e-mail marketer, one who is doing it the right way, has a separate e-mail for different lists.

✓ Recommended delivery frequency of E-mail campaigns: The deliver frequency of your e-mail campaigns heavily depends on the type of business. 90% of businesses need only send a monthly newsletter and the occasional events announcement but more often to share a weekly sale, or a daily special with coupons and discounts.

41. E-mail marketing is an amazing, sure-fire lead generator

✓ Make sure to include the forward to a friend button in the e-mail newsletter

✓ Entice people to join your e-mail list with a free gift like a relevant PDF document

✓ Set the auto responder to automatically send a welcome e-mail to new list members.

✓ Set the auto responder to send regular e-mail tips that are delivered weekly, biweekly or as often as you want

✓ Use your e-mail service provider reporting tools to measure how many leads were generated from e-mails

✓ Guarantee interactivity in your e-mails by including videos and hyperlink keywords and pictures

✓ Integrate e-mail, newsletters and social media by using the built in social media integration features

✓ Make e-mail marketing a part of your content marketing strategy with an integrated approach. It will save you time and generate traffic and clients

✓ Constant Contact is excellent for small business owners and entrepreneurs. Sign up today http://www.constantcontact.com/index.jsp?pn =thesnccway

Appendix A

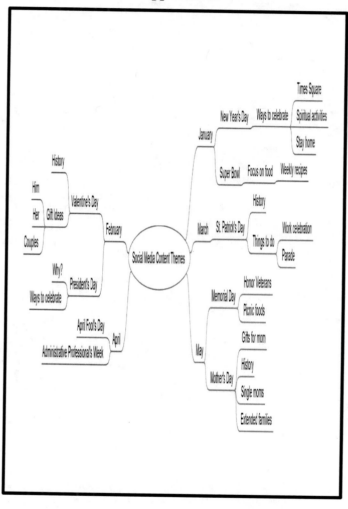

References

Preface

- Evanston, Ann and Landry, Lisa Ann: *Strategies for Marketing Successfully in Social Media.* https://www.udemy.com/strategies-for-marketing-successfully-in-social-media

Chapter Two: The Content Marketing Imperative

- Scott, David Meerman: *The New Rules of Viral Marketing: How word-of-mouse spreads your ideas for free*, 2008.

Chapter Three: The Fundamentals of Content Marketing and Social Media

- Advanced Marketing Institute http://aminstitute.com/headline/

- The Best Artists: *David and the Bad Block.* https://100swallows.wordpress.com/2008/02/04/david-and-the-bad-block/
- Draper, Grant: *Writing and Readability Scores-It Matters.* http://www.marketingprofs.com/articles/2014/12377/writing-and-readability-scores-it-matters
- Levine, Meridith: *10 Videos to Watch to Understand the Culture of Youtube.* http://blog.zefr.com/10-videos-to-watch-to-understand-the-culture-of-youtube/ Published January 7, 2014
- Pindoriya, Vishal: *Create Your Google Business Page or Risk Being Left Behind.* http://sendible.com/insights/create-your-google-business-page-or-risk-being-left-behind/ Published January 29, 2013
- Twitter. Wikipedia. https://en.wikipedia.org/wiki/Microblogging
- Twitter: http://science.opposingviews.com/purpose-twitter-12292.html
- YouTube: http://static.googleusercontent.com/external_content/untrusted_dlcp/www.youtube.com/en/us/yt/advertise/medias/pdfs/brand-channel-onesheeter-en.pdf

Chapter Four: Create a Marketing Strategy

- Albee, Ardath: *Up Close & Persona.*
  http://www.formstack.com/forms/?i-1064871-
  31curQ0CRT
- America's Funniest Home Videos.
  http://afv.com/about-the-show/
- Buyer Persona: *The Definition of a Buyer Persona [in Under 100 Words].*
  http://blog.hubspot.com/marketing/buyer-persona-definition-under-100-sr)
- Halvorson, Kristina: *Brain Traffic—Content Strategy for the Web.*
- Memmott, Mark. *Jedi? Vulcan? Mind Meld? Mind Trick? What Was Obama Thinking?*
  http://www.npr.org/sections/thetwo-way/2013/03/01/173251266/jedi-vulcan-mind-meld-mind-trick-what-was-obama-thinking
  Published March 1, 2013
- Redsicker, Patricia: *First Things First—Content Strategy Before Social Strategy.*
  http://contentmarketinginstitute.com/2011/05/content-strategy-before-social-strategy/
- Mindmap Defined:
  https://en.wikipedia.org/wiki/Mind_map

Chapter Five: Steps to Identify Keywords

- Adams, Chelsea: *What Are Keyword?*
  http://www.bruceclay.com/newsletter/volume113/
  what-are-keywords.htm Published May 23, 2013

Chapter Six: How to Improve Content Marketing
with Edgy Hashtags

- Bunskoek, Krista: *3 Key Hashtag Strategies: How to Market your Business & Content*
  http://blog.wishpond.com/post/62253333766/3-key-hashtag-strategies-how-to-market-your-business
- LePage, Evan: *The Do's and Don'ts of How to Use Hashtags*: http://blog.hootsuite.com/how-to-use-hashtags/ Published August 27, 2014
- Hashatit. https//www.hashatit.com
- Hashtags Staff: *Quick Start to Hashtags.*
  https://www.hashtags.org
- https://ritetag.com
- Keyhole. http://keyhole.co
- Wikipedia: Definition of an editorial calendar.
  http://en.wikipedia.org/wiki/Editorial_calendar

Chapter Eight: The Simple Truth about How to Keyword Optimize Your Titles and Content

- Dean, Brian: *Google Ranking Factors Checklist.* http://backlinko.com/google-ranking-factors. Published December 21, 2015
- Vavrek, Adam: *The Best Blog Titles for Your Content: 6 Best Practices for How to Get the Click.* Published July 3, 2012

Chapter Nine: A Remarkable KISS: Keep It Simple Success Model to Social Writing

- Burgstone, Jon and Murphy, Jr., Bill: *Why Customer Pain is Your Most Important Resource.* http://www.fastcompany.com/1844165/why-customer-pain-your-most-important-resource Published July 31, 2012
- Landry, Lisa Ann: *The S.M.A.R.T Rule for Using Social Media.* https://www.linkedin.com/pulse/smart-rules-using-social-media-lisa-ann-landry (Published January 16, 2015)
- Wikipedia. Call to Action Definition. https://en.wikipedia.org/wiki/Call_to_action_(marketing) Published November 9, 2015.

Chapter Ten: Publish Content with Appropriate Frequency and Length

- SlideShare Defined:
  http://www.slideshare.net/about
- Starak, Yaro: *What is a Podcast?*
  http://www.entrepreneurs-journey.com/230/what-is-a-podcast/
- Webopedia. Webinar Defined:
  http://www.webopedia.com/TERM/W/Webinar.html
- Wikipedia. Instagram Defined:
  https://en.wikipedia.org/wiki/Instagram
- Wikipedia. Pinterest Defined:
  https://en.wikipedia.org/wiki/Pinterest

Chapter 11: No! E-mail Marketing is Not Dead! It's Part of the Content Marketing

- CAN-SPAM Act: *A Compliance Guide for Business.*
  https://www.ftc.gov/tips-advice/business-center/guidance/can-spam-act-compliance-guide-business
- Constant Contact: *E-Mail Deliverability.*
  http://www.constantcontact.com/features/email-deliverability

- Devaney, Tim and Stein, Tom: *Why E-mail Is Still More Effective Than Social Media Marketing.* http://www.forbes.com/sites/capitalonespark/2013/10/01/why-email-is-still-more-effective-than-social-media-marketing/ Published October 1, 2013.
- Kelly, Murphy Samantha: *Study reveals how many times you should be checking e-mail daily to reduce stress.* (Published December 12, 2014)
- Paquet, Miranda: *Cheat Sheet 12 Ideas for Super Subject Lines.* http://blogs.constantcontact.com/ideas-for-subject-lines/?cc=SM_GG_ConstantContact Published July 21, 2015.

ABOUT THE AUTHOR

Do you need an *original, enterprising and forward-thinking* individual for your training initiatives and development needs? With spontaneity and a quick wit Lisa Ann Landry captivates audiences she trains and coaches. Her focus on higher standards and adding value through better execution enables her to rapidly earn respect as a corporate trainer, social media marketing trainer and business career coach.

Lisa Ann Landry has over 20 years of experience as a corporate trainer. She delivers skill enhancing, entertaining, and informative programs engaging audiences from start to the finish. One of her strengths is the ability to relate difficult concepts like how to use social media marketing in a way that the audience easily understand and can quickly apply. She gains immense satisfaction from her tenacity to conquer difficult content and capably teach it.

Today Lisa Ann Landry is a coach and international corporate trainer on variety of soft skills topics. She specializes in social media marketing. She teaches online courses and also delivers instructor led programs. Driven by a profound sense of adventure and creativity she is able to leverage creativity and cutting-edge thinking in the social media marketing arena. In addition to soft skills topics such as management and leadership, she teaches topics including Facebook, Google+, LinkedIn, Blogging, Twitter and social media marketing strategy for small business.

When you hire Lisa Ann Landry as a corporate trainer or as a social media strategist you receive top quality training curriculum and classroom training. Her instructor-led delivery will energize your staff with new applicable career skills that meet learning objectives. She's available as a career coach, corporate trainer and social media marketing strategist. Hire her to channel these uncommon talents in the training department and organization to guide your staff in reaching ultimate career potential.